Joel

Life, death, and passing through

Collected Poems 1960 - 2020

Preamble

Life, death, observations, politics, nature, racism, abstract thoughts, people, animals, places – these are the main elements of this diverse collection of my poems.

I have had, to date, three books published, but poetry has provided me with an exquisite outlet for my angst and grief which reached a denouement on a November afternoon in 1983 when I was informed I had less than three months to live – the experience which I hope I have reflected accurately in the poem I chose by way of a Foreword to this book.

Re-reading my poems from the early 1960s, I am painfully reminded of just how deeply I was affected by living in South Africa during the rise and callous implementation of the Apartheid regime and then emigrating my family to safety, first to London then to Australia. My poetry provided me with both a release for my frustration at the injustices I witnessed as well as providing me with an opportunity to reprimand a tyrannical institution and its enablers.

Thanks to poetry, I was able to express the highs and the lows of my love life and the symphony of finding my soulmate.

As to the form of these poems, you would be right to assume I was somewhat obsessed with the Sonnet form with its demand for brevity and fixed rhyme scheme.

Finally, I have simply indicated the year in which I wrote each poem and have presented them in sequence.

I Still recall that afternoon

I still recall that afternoon
In late November as I sat
Across the desk from Dr Gloom;
He clearly did not want to chat
As he described my pending doom
And told me that my end was soon.

Although it happened years ago
It's still imprinted on or my brain
As if it was just yesterday
I lost all hearing, as in vain
I hoped he'd smile and hear him say
"I'm wrong, you still have years to go."

It's 2020 as I write
While all about me all the world
Is sitting on a precipice;
A virus strain has been unfurled
And threatens to envelope us
And no one has been spared this blight.

So every day is like that day -
That day is 1983
When I was told my time was up.
So far the fates have nurtured me,
And always somehow filled my cup,
And kept me safe upon my way.

I'm not so vain as to believe
I'll live forever and withstand
The constant challenges I face.
But this I know that while I live
I'll keep my options close at hand
And choose those acts I can embrace.

2020

Table of Contents

Dormant

The moments shared we knew had set us free,
When hand in hand we walked beneath the moon;
When our lips spoke the unsaid words of love,
When we watched stars reflected on the sea,
Simply felt each other - you and me;
Then time stood still, our hearts beat fast, in tune.
You made my words a song, despair a key,
My pain a nonsense, Yes! You welcomed me.
You filled your cravings while the thrill was young,
But when it ended you found someone new!
My heart is bare, my words can find no tongue,
My lips you sealed; my soul is melted through!
The road seems yours to tread to your desire,
Aware that you once lit a dormant fire.

1960

Attack!

He has to eat - his hunger's raw,
An outstretched branch and he are one,
A single shadow from the sun,
From which he scans the forest floor.
With eyes agleam and filled with lust,
With sinews stretching to their core,
His tongue anticipates the gore
He'll lick when he has made his thrust.
His waiting tail flips idly round,
Its sinuous and muscled form
Suggesting his inherent norm,
To strike and kill without a sound!
But now he spots a distant flash,
And starts to focus on the grass
Through which the last man soon will pass;
He listens as he hears them thrash,
From right to left and then to right;

His muscles gather as they strain,

With every sinew, every vein,

As he prepares to pounce and bite.

They pass beneath the bough,

His yellow eyes are wide and set;

He's ready now - but not quite yet -

There is a moment cats know how.

The branches quiver with his spring,

As silently he hits his mark;

His claws dig deep, he gives a bark,

He holds his prey, for now he's king.

But then a shot, a muted roar,

He tumbles off his short-lived prey.

So short and deadly was the fray,

It's said it evened out the score!

1960

The Philosophers

Drawn from every rank and file of life,
Different ages and of different kind;
Some of youth, others grey in years,
Keen to prove the mysteries of life,
Show its futile or its worth of strife;
Show our birth, our end, and what is mind.
Help us that elusive truth to find -
Cut through doubts with knowledge as the knife.
They declare they cannot solve our quest,
But their precepts make the road less rough;
What is real is what they all have guessed
Through ideas some clear some not enough;
Lift our thoughts and give us clarity
To perceive - and so more clearly see.

1960

The lonely sea

It's a wide and lonely sea –

And the moonlight on its face

Shivers like such molten glass.

The mirror of my mind

Sees its fragile future moved

By the tides within its depths

1961

The train

I am homeward bound from here to there
Through the wide and mesmerizing veldt;
Note the wheels click like a metronome
On the tracks made from an iron belt;
Smell the coalsmoke from the engine's dome,
Hear the monster chuff the silent air.
Ferried as I am along the way,
Now with time unwound and space unrolled
I can see how we embrace our fate:
Cautiously or otherwise quite bold,
Making what we can of our estate,
Hoping there is no end to this day.
But too soon this journey has to end
At the final station round the bend.

1961

To: Francoise De Guigne*

Written 4 August 1961

Across the waves that wash a distant shore,
A land of peace too often torn by war;
A star appeared by not too many seen,
To spread its glow upon the lofty screen.
Its brightness spread, and as it grew
It welcomed in the early morning dew.
But then it sped upon a lengthy flight,
At last to shine afar both day and night.
It heeds a call and once more must return,
Again, upon that distant shore to burn.
But though the years will fade away
Your soul will surely guide me every day.
A genius rare that knew both joy and tears,
Yet felt the omnipresent earthly fears.

The words and music from your fingers flowed,
The statues - bronze and marble - ever glowed:
The portraits and the landscapes all alive
Created by an inner guiding drive.
In these to ages are you ever bound,
Away from chains that bind one to the ground.
And when no more your guiding light I see,
You will be present - always close to me.
You gave to all of what you ever knew,
You shunned the false and welcomed what was true.
Your sword, your book - the baggage of a Man -
The keystone of this universal Plan.

1963

*My high school teacher and undying mentor

From my window

(with apologies to William Wordsworth)

How sixteen months have passed, all with the length
Of sixty-four long weeks! again I see
Your eyes beguiling me from distant shores
With a strange attraction; once again
I see your curved and sensual lips
That in the past on mine did firmly press
With passion strong and fierce and so connect
Our hearts amid the tumult all around.
The day is come when once again I pray
That you, in dreaming of the times ahead,
Will join me once again in sweet content.
And though I'm not quite sure just how you feel,
We'll once more join as one and lose ourselves
'mid joys renewed; and carry on despite
The words and actions of their blithe reproach,
To carry on anew, oblivious

To all the sorrows that did make us part;

It's what I pray for all the while!

Withal uncertain as to what the future holds,

Of longer days and much still longer nights,

I gaze out from my window to the stars,

And sit and wait for you, for you alone.

1961

Even in a crowd…

The most subjective act of all –
To die.
The only instant in a life
Of that which all men hate to be -
Alone.
Depending and dependence fade
The moment death the two negates;
In loneliness a minute makes
An hour.
The many questions asked are trite,
Nor are there any to reply;
For all of that which is to come
In part – or all eternity -
Is long.

1962

Consternation

The strips of sticky tar
That join the concrete blocks;
The ropes that bind the rocks
Beneath a cruel star.
The countless sightless eyes
Reflect the city's haste,
But not the squalid waste
Or heaps of plaintive sighs.
Atop the topmost spires,
The dreams of men remain,
And if they are mundane,
Become the fuel for fires.
Consumed by lust and greed,
All men on men will feed.

1962

Addict

The dull insensate beat
That hammers in the brain;
A pinprick in a vein
Accomplishes this feat,
And drives one to repeat
And so destroy the pain.
A substance in the mind -
The drug of memory,
Attains a victory
When all the senses bind:
Retreat is but to find
The way to misery.
Forever to the past
The present seeks to cast.

1962

Moth

Around the luring dazzling light
Intent to reach the inner flame
It circles – plays a waiting game –
This tiny creature of the night.

In boldness foolishly expressed.
Its powdery wings the white heat touch –
Enveloped in the fiery clutch
It seeks no more its puny quest.

Attracted by the distant Light,
In time the wise and foolish come –
To die or to be stricken dumb;
It matters not – they have a right.

The flame will always show its might
To us – the creatures of the night.

1962

Glassblower

A cumbrous mound of earth,
A furnace flaming, hot,
Conjoined within the pot
In bubbling, dancing mirth.
The liquid glass is poured,
And fashioned in the moulds;
The form that he then holds,
Is turned again and cored.
He blows into the hole,
To give the figure life:
A face to see the strife
And hands to hold the scroll.
It takes a simple fall,
To break against the wall.

1962

Vain recollection

Words that mean so much -
Spoken from the heart;
When the lights depart
Leave the hands to touch.

Scenes that prompt a tear,
Make the reason balk;
Those who try to talk
Cannot hide the fear.

All the past is fled -
Leaves now turn to dust;
Underneath the crust
Hidden are the dead.

When recollections fade
Loss is made more real;

Life cannot reveal

Moments in the shade.

Tethered to a single star,

Bounded by the earth -

All the real is dearth

That the senses bar.

1962

Marble Lost

With careful aim and practiced eye
Along the ground he let it roll –
The boys all saw it near its goal,
Within he gave a thankful sigh;
But then, like one about to die,
The marble fell into a hole!
The joyous years that come with youth
Are but a season in our lives
Intemperate, while pleasure thrives.
Too late we realise the truth,
And so pretend to seek the couth;
But then it's gone - the Cold arrives.
The youth we seek to keep alive
Becomes a lifelong futile drive!

1962

The man who paused

A man was walking down the street,
A wrinkled frown upon his brow;
His eyes were fastened to his feet,
His steps were guided by the flow.

The traffic rolled and rumbled past
Still moving - whether slow or fast.

And at the traffic light he paused,
To wait for red to turn to green;
A fleeing car that wasn't seen –
A puzzle how his fall was caused?

The traffic rolled and rumbled past
Still moving - whether slow or fast.

In coffee bars and street cafes,

The talk on death went round and round:

Some said he had his Maker found,

And others stopped the passing trays!

The traffic rolled and rumbled past

Still moving - whether slow or fast.

The burial - that soon took place -

Attended only by the paid;

A little while the puzzled stayed

And frowned upon each other's face.

The traffic rolled and rumbled past

Still moving - whether slow or fast

Beside the sidewalk where he stood,

A patch upon the tarmac lies;

No more attended by the flies,

But only by a bloodied hood.

The traffic rolled and rumbled past

Still moving - whether slow or fast.

1962

The Tramp

He sits upon a bench and waits,
His vacant eyes just stare;
He hears the sounds of young debates,
And smells the scented air.

The crowd has risen to its feet,
He smiles upon the roar;
He never knew the word defeat -
And how his hopes did soar.

The taxi cabs and neon lights,
A hint of French perfume;
The wonders of those fancy flights -
And how did he presume.

The organ sounds that matched his pace,

A gesture on his arm;

The flawless, wan, and sculptured face -

And how he loved her charm.

The flying bombs and pleading screams,

A ruined and shattered world;

The day they lifted off the beams -

And how his feelings swirled.

The day he walked out on the street,

And sought the friends he knew;

He ran along with leaden feet -

But what he found was new.

The shadows stretch across the park,

The children have gone home;

He sees that soon it will be dark -

For now, his eyes just roam.

1962

Progress

Time to buy some flowers
Place them on a tombstone;
Mutter words of sorrow,
Quickly, call a taxi.

Gravel muffles noises
Even from the buried.

Wolfing toast and coffee
Saves the morning's minutes;
Read the blurry paper
Say hello to Johnny.

Pictures from an album
Found among the garbage.

Chronic heart disorders,

Duodenal ulcers,

Fills the daily columns -

Stories in the papers.

Once, when we were younger

We enjoyed the errands.

Scratching at the dinner,

Rushing to engagements,

In the stolen hours

Seeking every pleasure

Simple childhood wonders

Each one just as thrilling.

Time to change the flowers

(Taxis are expensive0;

Lots of time tomorrow

Then, they don't remember.

Planning for the future –

For a polished coffin.

1962

Orange blossoms

The breathless evening air,
Across the silent lake;
A world without a care,
That only gods could make.

The lofty hills around
Reflect the setting sun;
It fades without a sound –
In silence day is done.

The orange blossoms scent
The senses deeply drug;
While all desires consent
To drink from Heavens jug.

And now a star appears,

A world reborn anew;

And to the night endears

The deep and azure blue.

Like clouds of hazy white

A million jewelled stars

Adorn the velvet night

These fragrant words to parse.

The heart of love surrounds

Affinity of minds;

And into one compounds

The best of nature's finds.

1962

Pilgrim

Across the wild and stormy seas,

From port to port the sailors roam;

And he that seeks a single home

Must be content to hold the breeze.

The starting port still has its call,

And ever strives to hold its sway -

To alter speed and change the way

Would make the sails go slack and fall.

The harbour filled with coloured sail,

When left behind is ever gone;

The many lights that once had shone

At night the heavens still regale.

A haven found within the heart.

Is safety even when apart.

1962

Lines

The being of the not
The knot of being not;
Nor the being not
Of the being being not;
A moment undefined
Between the living-dead
The empty cold sick dread -
An empty thought confined;
Without a body - mind
Without a mind is dead.
The present is the past
That is the future too...
Being of a not-in-being,
Time unending ever seeing.

1962

On first understanding of William Blake

Imagination All -

Unbounded by a time or space;

Eternity a face

That turns around a see-through wall.

Reason - human scourge?

The power lifting man beyond

A puny mortal bond,

Is thought to be a doleful dirge.

The future, present, past,

Are but the moments of the whole -

As black as buried coal,

And death an angler's lucky cast.

The vale of daily life -

In which there is but little ease,

Where breath is but a breeze

Disturbing Death's amoral knife.

His words of vision then

Describe the world about me now;

Ease my furrowed brow,

To ponder on a common pen.

1962

Remorse

The residue, the sour taste -
Remorse, the cancer of the soul;
The memory that lingers on
That only now reveals the truth -
It’s compensation for a loss,
Where heightened passions sought a cure
To still the rising flood of need.
A moment's indiscretion rests
Oblivious to any tears;
The mute orgastic future’s dreams
That link the present to the past -
When Reason hides behind a cloud
All facile feelings wander free,
And seek refuge in distant thrills.
The moon that rises in the West
Becomes the bane of silent nights -

And that which seemed to fill the void

Is but a vacuum lacking life.

Remorse remains to wait the day

When once again it feeds the pain.

1962

Antithesis

Tinder dry and empty,
Hollow pipes,
Sunk below the surface
Under ice cold marble.

Rooms of overwhelming blackness;
All with doors that have no handles;
Flesh that feels like molten candles -
Waxy, brittle, weak and bloodless.

Bones forever buried,
Cracked and crumbling –
Rotting in the bowels,
Turning grey and musty.

Walls with heavy woollen wadding,
Held by slender metal wires;

Gripping blunted cutting pliers,

Mad Frustration bangs the padding!

Carbon-copied faces -

Smiling deadly:

Passions, fears are ended,

Death can have no feeling!

1962

Spring rain

The long and languid nights and days,
The dry and dusty dying earth -
A season marked by verdant dearth
Is gone - without a word of praise.
Spring-rain! A soft and warm refrain
That rises to a driving theme,
Then spreading to a gentle stream
Brings joy once more to hearts in pain.
Warmth is seen in children's faces,
Lovers' glances and the aged;
In the leaves that seem so faded –
Strains of dear remembered places.
In the Season's first expression
Surely lies the Resurrection!

1962

Displaced

What thoughts attend on mortal man
Are but the foibles to his acts;
Conjecture rouses doubtful facts
Yet seems the while to fit the plan;
Imagination is the glue;
For as the reason power gains,
And passion to its utmost strains,
It's force of will that takes one through.

For when the day comes to an end,
The heart of man rejoins the night -
And there remains a star in flight,
A part of which he is a blend;
Imagination must suspend
The reason - passions rest alone,
By will into the action sown -
On only these can man depend.

The fate of man himself must seek,
And to his Self remain confined;
The moments that are undefined,
Are as a man that cannot speak -
Frustrated and forever weak:
The peace that seems to lie without,
Remains a fear that one must flout,
If not - then turn the other cheek!

1962

Thoughts

A thought contained and unexpressed
Is as the moment after life -
Completely dead.
And as the leaves
That in the Autumn turn to brown,
A part of that which has to die.

A man who lives inside his head
Who cannot tell the what from why
Is also dead -
A drifting shell
Asleep upon a silent sea
Beneath the curtain of the night.

A child unborn, a thought stillborn,
Are so like bodies in a tomb,
Removed from death.

Attached to life

We're born to bear the agony

Of waiting for the final shock.

A road unguided and unsigned

Will turn the traveler away

To find himself

To lose his self

Somewhere among the fenceless fields

Criss-crossed with unseen paths.

A life unlived is as a death:

You cannot grieve for what's not known

Or what will never be.

And we are dead

If all the thoughts we think we think,

Have somehow yet to be expressed.

1963

Prison

The walls are made of fears,
The bars of empty hopes;
And where the spirit gropes
There is no place for tears.
The smooth and granite floors,
The dampness rank as sweat,
And as the passions fret
The passing hours pause.
The door is made of life,
The lock of broken dreams;
Eternity it seems
Is found within this strife.
The bread is sour love,
The water rancid joys;
And here where men are boys
The glories lie above.
The labyrinth is this –

The anguish and the pain;
Privation and the gain –
The turnings which we miss.
The memories requite
The silence of the years;
Imagination sears
Where terror is the night.

1963

Feeble endeavour

What is beauty - that which men desire?
What is love - that trite and tender feeling?
What is it the passions are revealing
Ever adding lumber to the fire?
Beauty! Love! The words which spell destruction
Overwrought and fashioned by the carnal -
These will never destined for a charnel,
Nor for use in foolish deconstruction.
These are jaded dreams and as them fleeting,
But revealed in humble deeds and action
Lies the consummation of attraction
By the reason and the senses meeting.
Thoughts and feelings seeking explanation
Simple words can never give direction.

1963

There was a time

There was a time...

When there were men upon the earth,

And creatures in the forests dim;

And all around were sounds of mirth

And hearts that over-swelled the brim.

There was a time...

Amid the days of joyful glee,

When fret and fear were still unknown;

When limbs and every thought were free,

And seeds of pain were never sown.

There was a time...

The day you joined the battle cry

To wander in Elysium;

When death in life was not to die,

But fear of Pandemonium.

There was a time...

When there were men who still could love,

And find fair promise in a rose;

And truths that were not sought above

But in the warmth of still repose.

There was a time...

Amid the nights of awe and fear,

When men around the fires spoke;

When sudden joy could bring a tear,

And understanding love evoke.

There was a time...

The day has long since passed away,

To leave a quiet memory;

When yesterdays were not today

But just a waking reverie.

There was a time...

When there were instruments of pain

And mad devices just to kill;

When loss of glory was a bane,

And strength of thought was just a skill

There was a time...
Enow, when viewed in retrospect
The world - a horror from the grave,
When but to stand in still aspect,
Was just to be a silent knave.

There was a time...
When there were men upon the earth
And creatures in the forests dim,
But in the moment of their birth,
Came death that over-swelled the brim.

There is still the time...
1963

Drunk

I grabbed her by the neck
My hand upon her mouth,
I shouted, 'What the heck!'
And headed for the South*.
I propped her by a tree,
Untied my shoes and tie;
I felt quite cold and dry -
But this would give me glee.
My lips against her mouth -
It felt so warm and soft;
My spirits soared aloft
Ah! The burning South!
She looks so empty now,
And drained of all her strength;
I looked upon her length
And lowly mumbled 'Wow!'
I headed home alone

And feeling morbid too;

And so, my friend would you

If you had only known!

1963

- *Southern Comfort Whisky*

Recollections

The melancholy of a wind-swept thought
The bitter sweetness of a deep regret;
For tempered age in pain will not forget,
And Youth is chary of the things it ought.
So, in the image which the years have caught
We find expressed the dreams which hopes beget.
But all the splendours of the past are dead,
And what we still retain is what we will;
For we are children of the future still,
And are by dreams and wild emotions led.
How then to pacify the awful dread
That comes of memories we feel are chill?
The leaves we heap the wind will blow away,
For after Summer, Autumn too must play.

1963

Solitude

I walk along a barren shore,
I hear the rushing of the surf;
The waters swirl about my feet,
And on my head the stars wink down.

I see the lone and limpid moon -
The silver ribbon on the waves;
And so entranced by nature's spell,
I disregard the undertow.

A grain of salt upon the sand –
A corner in the universe;
The frailty of my human form
Is shadowed by my strength of thought.

Retracing footprints on the sand,
I keep on seeking for a path;

But all the dreams of yesterday
The passing tides have washed away.

To linger on the sand of life -
The narrow strip upon the brink;
A long and final backward glance,
The past that calls - the fate of Lot.
1963

The silent hawk

The mournful bleating of the lambs that cry
As sheep into the sunset slowly walk;
Above, the ever-watchful wheeling hawk –
A lonely silhouette against the sky.
A single lamb detaches from the flock,
And in a rush of wind is snatched away;
Unmoved the rest proceed upon their way -
So many carcasses of living stock.
At night they all are huddled in their pen,
Their only comfort one another's breath;
For what they fear is not the smell of death –
They fear the voices and the tread of men.
The dread that man can feel within his breast -
The silent hawk now resting in his nest.

1963

Children of the dark

Amid the shrinking circle of this life,
Amid this world so torn with human strife,
Some moments still reveal reality,
Those moments when we know that we are we.
But there are times when truth is just a dream
And all appears as we would have it seem;
As I, beside the table where I sit
I look across and see a vacant seat.
In hope I fill it with your laugh and smile
And then I talk to you for quite a while.
You laugh and smile and even talk to me;
But when I cry, I know you cannot see;
The vision disappears before my eyes –
Imagination born of all my sighs.
The single path we walk is long and hard
Behind the buildings all lie burnt and charred -
The shattered city of my broken past

Has lost the many members of its cast.

It's vain repeating long-forgotten pains,

They are indeed the very future's gains!

For all the agony that we have felt

Has left its mark just like an open welt;

The hopes that come from all my many dreams

I find forever bursting at the seams.

And now, awake upon my bed at night

The fear returns - again I shake with fright.

But you and I are children of the dark -

For now, it's just more present and more stark.

We reach across to touch but cannot find,

Of course! The truth is really in my mind.

1963

Witness

The sky above
The earth below
Would seem to know
It's you I love.

For in between
We are contained
As lovers pained
At what has been.

The sky above
The earth below –
How could they know
How much I love?

They gather storms
And heap up dust;

Then in a gust

Create new forms.

The sky above,

The earth below,

Will never know,

It's you I love.

1963

Stanzas

To love is for a love to be expressed
In deed, and not as other moods, suppressed;
For when expounded in three syllables
In time becomes a sum to be assessed.

But when the liquor of the heart turns chill,
And tears for no apparent spill,
Then comes the time to waive the former choice
And seek another even greater thrill.

So why pretend that passions still run hot
When they have cooled and hardened like a clot?
For love that wanes despite all vain attempts
At clutching at a hope, becomes a blot.

Some say, "what happens does so for the best,"
And some, "Why fret? All love and life's a jest;"

But when complete surrender has been made
What happens is what only fools request.

So, say, "Surrender not your inner soul,
For when you do you split your very whole."
Yet what are words in matters such as this,
When you insist on keeping up your role?

The age of youth is as the age of old -
When even though ideals we try to hold
Like liquid through our fingers ever seep
In vain endeavours to remain as bold.

To love belongs not to the old or young
Who have not yet the cloths of anguish wrung,
And dehydrated thus are more aware
That even this is nought when life is hung.

A love, as life, must turn the circle round,
And as it started, end; or else resound
With cries of nights completely unfulfilled
And days that disappeared without a sound.

But you, because you are, and what you are
Must needs be otherwise; so as a star
You will remain untouchable, and seen
As such, be yet desired though so far.

Some sages disagree about the truth
Of what is real or merely dreams, but youth
Unlearned has yet to think, it acts and lives
According to the call; Is that uncouth?

Agree that we are children, you and I,
So why pretend to be adult? We vie
For all of that which is beyond our ken –
For what? A child thinks not that life will die.

The passions are as fruits that we can taste
Or place in jars; but let them turn to waste
And see how soon the moss upon them grows:
How say you this is what is meant as 'chaste?'

In stumbling through the darkness of this life
We nonetheless all seek a light; yet rife
Will be the many lamps we do not seek,

The hands unfelt before the mortal knife.

But should you stagger into what appears
To be a lamp, allay your present fears
For just awhile - and hold not fast, instead
Just lean against it lightly with the years.

And those who clutch at love with all their might
Grow faint with fear that it will take to flight;
For just as life it is a nightingale
That sings awhile, and then embraces night.

1963

Strangers all

The things we see around us every day -
The many things we seek to understand;
For we have lived amid another land
And in this maze we cannot find our way.
We stop the many people on the street -
Our fellow travelers on this unknown road;
But then they too, like us, have thither flowed
And cannot tell us where the crossroads meet.
As they, we stand and ever gaze beyond,
And in our endless anguish wait for Truth;
But we have long since left the paths of youth,
And now are but the stragglers demi-monde.
And still we think we are, and are,
But as we burn, we find that we still char.

1963

The end

The world stood still at last -

The heart that throbbed had ceased;

For every man and beast

The life to be had passed.

The hot and burning tears,

The overflowing grief,

For there is no relief

From all the fading years.

We follow like the sheep

Behind the Judas goat;

And when they cut out throat

We fall and bleed to sleep.

Completely blind and dumb -

Insensitive to life -

The wielder of the knife

Is just as shocked and numb.

A day or two will pass -

And they will seem like years;

The nights will hold no fears

And we will simply pass.

1963

Execution

Standing bound and gagged...waiting…

Staring forward into nothing;

Hoping vainly just for something -

Anything to end the anguish.

You are certain it is summer,

For the spring came after winter;

You had also seen the blossoms

Turn to fruit, mature and ripen.

Now you hear the thud of rifle

Butts resounding on the concrete,

And the prison's awful silence

Just before an execution.

Now the final words are given ...

Suddenly your eyes turn upward,

Light! The mask has slipped a little -

Smile, you know the order, "Fire!" 1963

The party

Empty glasses on the tables,
Brandy sloshed upon the ceiling.
All is silent save the sighing

Of the curtains as the morning
Breezes filter through the windows;
Yes, the party's long since ended.

Names and corresponding faces
Blur before my hazy vision;
But the flower in my fingers

Is distinct and still quite fragrant -
It belonged (I think) to someone.
But the party's over... is it?

1963

Condemned

An interlacing iron grille
Casts slab of moonlight one by one;
But on the distant concrete roof -
A hazy image two by two.
An interplay of light and shade -
The pattern of the nights and days;
We walk the dungeon of the years
Above, below this heavy grate.
And in the black and moonless nights -
The stifling silence of the dark,
The mute oppressiveness of fear
That stars are merely mirrored hopes.
And then the light of dawn appears -
Reveals a window - burglar proofed!

1963

Evening star

The blue white fire of the evening star
Now glimmers through a silky veil
Of pearly gold and burnished rust –
The parting banner of the setting sun.
And over all the fading black green trees,
And sloping roofs of sun-baked tiles,
The russet mantle slowly spreads –
A dullish glow of dying pallid red.
A squeaking bat swoops by and is perplexed
By knowing not which way to turn -
The neon lights have all been powered on
To light the dark and sleepy avenues.
Above me high I hear a distant roar
And see the alternating lights –
An aeroplane about to land
Upon a violet-lighted landing strip.
Now down the street I hear the sound of feet

Of weary workmen trudging home;

Their voices pierce the sullen gloom

Reminding me that that people live near here.

The lazy sounds of night are louder now -

The crickets, beetles and the bats;

And still I see the evening star

Alone, against the dark it seems more bright.

1963

Remembrance

Through the spring of expectation,
Through the autumn of foreboding,
Comes the winter of remembrance
That embraces all the seasons;
Best remembered is the summer –
Life amid a time of reaping.
This the youth - the sad remembrance
For the scent of orange blossoms,
For the lovers of the evening,
For the wine of all our passions,
For a brush against the petal
As it sheds its powdered fragrance.
But beneath the sands of passing
There is nothing - only absence.

1963

Smithy

We are fashioned on the anvil
Of our hopes and disappointments;
Yet we never seek the reason
For the odd resulting figure.

Some will quiz the dusky blacksmith,
Some will poke around the embers,
Some will scrutinise the hammer,
Some the marks upon the anvil.

From our painful birth we suffer,
And we all remain disfigured;
Why then seek out what is perfect
If it's just a misconception?

Born to death we loiter... waiting...
Never ceasing for the moment

To anticipate the ending

Or deny complete acceptance.

Life is in the very living,

And the scars that it engenders;

It is we who wield the hammer -

All the rest is accidental.

1963

Sparrow

I saw a Sparrow in a tree,

And then I saw a butcher bird;

So busy was he watching me

He could not even dare look up.

I waved my arms and made a noise -

Confused the issue and his flight.

Now there he lies upon on the ground,

His feathers broken - and his heart.

The very self-same tree is there,

The sky above is just as blue,

But I am older, sadder now,

And see no sparrow in a tree;

Yet when I lie awake at night

I hear him calling... calling… me?

1963

Prayer

He knew him by his other name,

His deeds and thoughts he heard hearsay;

Was he to frown or even doubt

The sayings of the worldly wise?

The gates they said are made of gold,

The fields beyond are Evergreen;

It never rains that side of Hell

Where even moonbeams are not cold.

Your loves and dreams will all emerge,

To weep will be because of joy;

Your bed will be bedecked with stars,

And sleep will be a self-repose.

The peace that's hidden in your mind

Will be as soothing to your form;

Eternity awaits your call –

The finest of the sweetest choice.

He knew him by his former name,

And what he heard was still hearsay

Yet he is doomed this side of Hell -

He wants to live, and they are dead.

1963

I weep for you

I weep for you -

The sunlight which the stars have crossed

Between the galaxies of thought;

Amid the dreams of fancy lost

There lies the Will I ever sought.

I weep for you –

The carefree joyous days of Youth

That form the oft-remembered past;

The foundry which exists uncouth

In which the present dies were cast.

I weep for you -

The traveller in the maze of life

Perplexed by all its subtleties;

Forever torn by worldly strife

And human disabilities.

I weep for you –

The innocence which man has lost

And found replaced by earthly greed;

For though the sun can melt the frost

It reaches not the buried seed.

I weep for you –

The rose and lily in the fields

Which men destroy to plant the rye;

For he that still the sickle wields

Anon will find that men too die.

I weep for you -

The lover with his tales of woe

And dreams atop a garbage can;

I shudder when the breezes blow –

For in my anguish, I am Man.

I weep for you –

The poet and the man of arms

Deployed among the scattered ranks,
Where each of you has found his charms
On foaming steeds with steaming flanks.

I weep for you –
The children of this Iron Age
Grown old and long before your time;
For speed now obviates the stage
When thoughts of man should be sublime.

I weep for you –
The poor and all the very rich,
The ones in fact who are bourgeois;
For in the soft and fresh-dug ditch
Is no discernible patois.

I weep for you –
The babes and men about to die –
The silent poised above the brink;
Beneath the waves the timeless lie
And wait for Man they know must sink.

I weep for you –

Who breathe and yet do not exist,
Are but the very living-dead;
For on the sensual do subsist
The corpses which the reason fled.

I weep for you -
The ones who thrive on other souls
You wish to save before the grave;
To hand out all the empty doles,
And then in Jordan's waters lave.
I weep for you.

1963

Too late

The marble slabs beneath the leaden sky
With wistful words of woe thereon inscribed;
The sole reminders of a life described -
The acres where the unremembered lie.
Reminded, some remember, then they cry -
The moments which their consciences prescribed.
If death be just a servant of our fears,
Remembrance then can be a soothing balm;
For what we fear can do us mortal harm
Unless erased by weeping floods of tears;
And of the dead we knew in distant years
To weep enow will augur greater calm.
We grieve not for the living but the dead -
In this we are to blame for all our dread.

1963

Trapped

Within the dark and musty cells,
With bars instead of windowpanes;
Where all is dark perpetually
The inmates of this hell just sit.
Oblivious to all outside,
They sit in silence in the gloom;
Surrounded by the trowelled walls
Reflecting nothing of themselves.
Like figures in a gallery -
So many waxen effigies
Just gazing blankly as if blind;
For though they look they cannot see.
The many whispered sounds are heard,
That float as from the nether world;
Forever present "on the other side" -
But like the ghosts they are they fade.
With greed they eat the self-same food,

They love, and when in anger, fight;
And when the Warder's steps are heard
Resume their seats and fearing - wait.
Beyond their walls is mystery,
And though they contemplate escape
Remain - for all the fears beyond
They think will lead them back to hell.
And so they pass their lives away
Contained within their worldly cells -
The cells that turned to corridors
Down which their final steps must go.
1963

Natural Death

The swinging gallows and the deadly noose,
The wooden trapdoor in the concrete floor;
The oval chamber made of stainless steel
With portholes for the viewers all around.
The solid sheet of highly razored steel
That rests between the uprights highly oiled;
The padded chair with dangling wires straps
Electrified, to shock, to stun, and kill.

The bullet-riddled, pock-marked bloody walls,
The white-hot shrapnel from the bursting bombs;
The flaming petrol spilled from Molotov's -
All these and more - the instruments of war.

To die and know the very reason why
The end that comes is but a passing phase;
Eternity is that which lies beyond the grave

For those who from this very life escape.
It matters not if one is very old
Or in the bloom of years still fresh and gay;
Except perhaps when one is still alive
The fear to leave all this behind is strong.

But what is this? This endless chain of death
That stretches from the womb unto the grave;
The life that is the linking interlude -
The night that comes between the dusk and dawn?
And in the shadows of the gathering gloom
What shapes appear before the dimming eyes -
Are like so many old remembered things,
And yet unlike them in their ghostly form.

Upon a single mask at once is seen
The dying soldier and the man condemned;
The man dependent on the surgeon's knife,
The puny helpless babe at birth stillborn.

The many ways of death are really one -
And therein lies the greatest fear of man;
For when the agony or peace have gone

The long unknowing endless sleep begins.

Today, and all tomorrows, yet to come,

Eventually remain the yesterdays.

Remembered for a while by those we loved

And who, in turn, become remembered, too.

1963

Paradise

The day you left without a word,
The sun took on a wintry chill;
The dew upon the windowsill
The long cold day inferred -
In retrospect it's all absurd;
And in my populated mind
No answers can my reason find -
The weak of man again incurred.

The heavens gape, asunder split,
Unleash with thunder all their force -
The fury of a storm is coarse;
Its strength against the lull to pit,
No man can ever dare outwit.
The bluebird and the peaceful dove,

Epitomise the tranquil love -
Utopia - or just a bit?

The seven wonders of the world,
With joy the hearts of men once filled;
And bubbling o'er the walls were spilled
The waters that the gods had hurled,
And scenes of splendour were unfurled;
But now the buildings that abound,
The lofty thoughts of men confound
With structures of a brave new world.

To leave the third dimension far behind,
Upon imagination bound;
To enter, and without a sound,
The fourth - a paradise of mind
To which the passport Death has signed.
With you again I will be whole,
In body and eternal soul -
Alas! It's here I am confined!

1963

Apocalypse

They streak across the storm-lashed sky,
Astride the charred and glowing clouds;
Between the sheets of pillared flames,
And thermoplastic corridors.
Electric burning everywhere
Now mingles with the vapid air
While thundering and pounding hooves
Reverberate in endless swells
Until, at last, the senses die
Amid the fiery holocaust.
Foundations crumble at the core,
And topless towers topple down;
Crevasses scar the heaving fields,
And stony rubble all about
Impedes the flying frightened feet -
These silhouettes against the flames.
Belaboured breathing is now heard

From all the alleys in the dark -

The respite lasts for just a while

And then all hell breaks loose again.

The blood is splashed against the walls,

And screams of terror pierce the night;

Pursued by laughs maniacal

That echo off hollow walls

The hunted flee with quaking hearts.

The rattling deep machine-gun fire

Is lost amid the turbulence -

The horrible and deadly force -

The mass explosions in the sky.

A depthless silence lies about,

While from the broken windowpanes

(like the eyes of blinded people)

Drops of dark red blood still trickle…

The streets are dark abysses now,

And like the buildings, derelict;

Battered ships and fallen bridges

Lie askew about the harbour;

And through the mass of broken stones

That lie about the silent streets,

A hand is seen to twitch - then move.

1963

Dream of death

To run yet keep on standing still,
To feel a hand around your heart;
Escaping is a practised art
That only dreamers can fulfill.

The terrors of a painful dream –
A silent land with no escape;
A cell where prisoners have no shape,
Nor voices to express their scream.

To keep on falling down a well,
To fall, revolving down and down:
The mighty king and knavish clown
Are mixed up by the smoke of hell.

The passing dream and all its hosts –
The mirror of eternal night,

Of man in all his painful plight –

Of death and all its living ghosts.

1963

Three worlds

Dilapidated, dark and musty shacks,
The children playing in the pools of mud,
The alleys where the cats and vermin scud –
The area that lies beyond the tracks.
The yards where engines toot and billow steam;
Where all is wreathed in clouds of murky smoke -
A formless mass beneath a ragged cloak,
Encircled by a maze of cul-de-sacs.

The boulevards that run along the shore,
The zebra crossings' strips of black and white
Can seem the same when day has turned to night –
These zigzags that become an either, or:
Veneered – the faces and the flushed facades
Behind whose walls the greedy lusting thrives;
The dissolute unmotivated lives,
Where yells are drowned beneath an endless roar.

Pedantic pedagogues in stuffy rooms,

The preachers with their smirking mirthless smiles;

With flowered words to hide their many wiles,

They guide the unsuspecting to their tombs –

The weak that hardly ever brave themselves;

And pity both the poorly rich and blind -

The men who will not to their conscience bind

Responsibility that surely looms.

1963

Vain compromise

He sees the fading sun in flaming red,
And on the ground the heaps of fallen leaves;
His memory awakes and longing grieves
For all the blossoms and the fruit now dead;
He sees the stumps and barren boughs instead -
Can Nature thus its many loves deceive?
The silhouettes against the silver sky -
The branches, gaunt, grotesque and deathly still;
And all at once the air is rank and chill,
And darkness rests where heaps of leaves now lie.
He hears a distant trembling, plaintive cry -
Can Love but ever all of Nature fill?
A stranger in a land forever strange -
A shadow's shape that must forever change!

1963

No reply

All my dreams have been ignored -

Like a distant telephone

Ringing in a vacant house.

Such the unrequited pleas

Men have uttered through all time

To a high, indifferent sky.

1963

Paperweight

The universe of make believe,
The world of business and its 'charms';
The tiny plot that nurtures alms
Yet knows not of the words 'to grieve'.
An endless cycle made of guile,
Investments made of human fears;
And when the strain gives way to tears,
They hide behind a stony smile.
They designate the all by names,
And numbers then they classify -
But when the labels fade and die,
They find no answers to their claims.
This is the balance made by man,
To hold forever - if he can!

1963

Angst

Oh! If it was but tomorrow,
Not the anguish of this moment!
When a life amounts to nothing
It is like the muted future:
Possible and yet uncertain,
Crowded with imagination,
Silent in its void expression,
Dead until it meets the living.
Then would man forget his grieving,
Live a life of thought-in-action,
And instead of wild reaction,
Yield the fountain of his being,
Subjugate his realm of passions,
Serve his bold imagination.
Stitched together past and future
We are bound by our decisions,
Always searching for our freedom,

But restrained by time-in-motion;

This, the anguish of the moment,

This, the horror of our being.

1963

On looking at a flower

What life can you now see,
Detached from where you came?
For though you seem the same
I hear your silent plea.
Your soul too soon was killed,
And deep within you cry;
You did not want to die,
But fancy had you willed
To lie upon my hand
Where none had lain before,
To make my senses soar
Above this rocky land.
Your beauty wilts and fades,
Your heart has now run dry;
But in my heart I vie
For snatches of your shades.
The truth was in the thrill -

The pleasure that you gave;
To live is all I crave
As in your fashion - still.
Removed from lust and fear;
Aware of all around
You uttered not a sound
And shed a honeyed tear.
Now you are lost, alas!
Your love is not for men!
1963

Sublime cupidity

Both you and I are old -

Alas! We should be younger still;

But time is like a threshing mill

And we the waters cold.

A minute by the glass

Is all we ever understand;

We trickle through a timeless hand

And wonder as we pass.

We will be ageless still

(How vainly do we therefore grope!).

And though we think we know, we hope

To flower on the will.

If here the sands of time have lied -

We should be on the other side.

1963

Dusk

The land is quiet now;
The evening shadows spread -
Like inkblots of the dead
Upon the fading glow.
But then it must be so
Amid the silent graves,
The charnels of the slaves,
The men who pleaded "No!"
Yet only yesterday
A sunset was a thrill;
But blood must ever spill
If hell is every day.
The respite is the night -
The cavern filled with dread;
And here the living-dead

Forever wield their might.

So shut the gates of Hell -

The portals of our birth;

There is no joy or mirth

Within a winch-less well.

1963

Life

Man, in isolation
Seeking for his freedom
In the shadeless desert
Not the cruel city.
Lonely as a sandstorm,
Humble as a camel –
And then he realises –
Life is air and water.
Not the blood and torture,
Nor the peopled furnace,
But the quiet vision
Of the earth in motion.
Dust benumbs the senses,
Clouds the lofty image;
What remains is Reason
And a blissful silence.
Danger is still present,

Only *there* it matters;

Life can never conquer,

Courage being master.

Sand is universal,

There upon the desert,

One is unimportant -

Of this fact I'm conscious.

Freedom then this knowledge -

Life is not the living

Nor the after-dying;

Life is what is needed!

1963

The Warder's keys

Suspended by a waking dream,
I lie between two points in time;
And any thoughts which are sublime
My incapacities blaspheme.
To walk the corridors of Hell,
Between the many peopled walls,
And through the dark and vistaed halls
To find that none are parallel.
He walks behind me does the Ward,
Reminds me with a shake of keys
That we are dying by degrees,
And this is but the small reward.
At dawn the wooden trap is sprung,
By dusk the victim has been hung.

1963

What mirror?

The moon that shines by day
Reflects the sun that glows by night;
And stardust on the way.
Obscures the vision and the sight.
The rain falls up not down,
And raises sandstorms in the clouds;
While this deserted town
Depends upon its thronging crowds.
The woman giving birth
Performs her labour in the grave;
And all the sounds of mirth
Are uttered only by a slave.
Like this we dream the truth on earth,
And which, by living, waive.

1963

Volcano

The flaming rivers in the night
Explode and char the leafless trees -
Ignite the hot and breathless breeze
Revealed the chaos to the sight.

A land of choking sulphur fumes
Beneath the sky of glowing clouds;
Of panic-stricken screaming crowds -
And still the mad volcano spumes.

The night it seems has passed away
Before the grey and smoking East;
Now there is neither man nor beast
To greet the coming of the day.

The course of every dying thing

Revolves and dies a little more -
Conceals the inner fears that gnaw -
Allows the gods a while to sing.

At once a green and living land,
At once a charred and dying field;
But then to die is but to yield
Forever to the life at hand!
1963

Children

In the distance I can see

Children walking on a wall

Using clouds for handlebars.

Like the adults they'll become

Stumbling indecisively

On the thin edge of the world.

1964

Epitaph

You'll write your name in blood
Across the deserts of the world,
When mingled with the grains of sand
That trickle through the hourglass
The tale of man will then be told.
It will not be an anecdote
Or one of syllables disjoined;
But as the River of the Shades
Will flow unbroken and undammed.

When all the earth lies charred and scarred,
When all the birds have ceased to sing,
A man will write his name in blood
Across the deserts of the world.
He will be unlike any man;
A figure tempered by his wit,
Dispassionate in deed and thought,

As free as dreams that have no form,

And known as only I can know.

1964

Wistful thoughts

Can wistful thoughts evoke the sunset's glow?
The crimson sea at dawn's first light,
The silver moon upon its starry flight,
The times when seeing these we somehow know
That what we see and love for now must go;
The fear we hide that this is just a dream
Or that eventually it all will seem
That we were viewers of a fancy show?
A cold wind rustles through the trembling leaves
And sheds their burnished leaves upon the ground
Where they now lie, and no one ever grieves
For they have fallen where there is no sound.
O memory! Can you be ever true
Revive the faded scenes I know I knew?

1964

Thoughts

The months gone by have mellowed thoughts
That once had seemed too full to bear,
But now an absence mute and chill
Is felt, and thoughts of brown still live.
For thoughts unburdened, passions, too,
Are doomed to live without an end.
The lighter load is born of acts
That once expressed will surely die,
Not in the present but in dreams.
Is my reality confused?
For now, it seems that men are still,
The elements and Nature speak.
The contemplation of a thought –
A memory and vision fused.

1964

Missing

It's all so very quiet, lonely, still,
In that secluded place I know so well
Must be the wild antithesis of hell
Which even life transfused can never fill.

A line omitted on a filled-in page,
A break among the rumbling clouds of wrath
A meadow with a vein of dying swath
A time which now no longer harbours age.

The words that should have been but were not said,
The life so full that clearly was not filled,
The fluid passions that were never stilled,
The life to which our reference was the dead.

It's not so far to walk if you have feet,
Nor hard to see if you have open eyes;

But being victims as we are of sighs

Our efforts cannot be but incomplete.

The awful subjectivity of things

No more than shadows in the shrouded haze;

And when there are no more of nights and days

Be pleased you will no longer pray for wings!

1964

Game of life

The cards have all been dealt
Face down; all eyes look down to see,
And seeing not, look up
Expectantly with open mouths.
The silence hangs in drops
Of perspiration on their brows;
Some shift uneasily
And others gaze with staring eyes.
If only one would call…
He will! The others he will lead
And they, in turn, will bid
And play according to his will.
And when the cards at last are stacked
They all will be the first to leave!

1964

Lines

A small intrigue

A little fear,

A little tear –

Oh, such fatigue!

The niceties,

The wounding word,

It's all absurd

The things we seize!

1964

Landscape

The wooded slopes in neat array
That lean against the mountains blue,
The firs and pines in shades of green -
Of colours always looking new.
The lighting of the sky's wide screen
Denotes the coming of the day.
A closer glance at once reveals
A wooden cabin and a stream,
And children playing in the nude –
A far cry from the human teem
In towns and cities closely queued,
Where people shop for store-front deals.
The gallery must close at eight
And leave me to my urban fate!

1964

A Poem

In a poem there is heart,
Moving as the rhythm of
Water over pearly stones
Flowing to the larger sea.
In a poem there is soul,
Floating as the silent clouds
White upon a sky of blue,
Soaking in eternity.
In a poem there is life,
Phrased in subtle shades of thought;
Waving willows in the heat
Under which relief is cool.
As the things which hurt and kill
In a poem there is death.

1965

Stolen Fruit

To steal along an orchard wall,
A leap and then to snatch some fruit;
Disheveled in his Sunday suit,
He flees regardless of the call.
He enters through the choir door,
Unnoticed joins in hymns of praise;
How blissful are those endless days
Of stealing fruit and wanting more!
The orchard and the fruits are gone –
Alone amid the wooden pews
He sees the poplars and the yews,
And wonders if the sun had shone.
His life is now a memory,
His gain the pain of reverie.

1965

On the passing of a cousin

Have you ever seen a line of people
At a distance, still, and strangely silent;
While the oaks and pines behind them swaying
Seem like ghosts performing incantations?

Granite slabs of ashen, angled tombstones
Bear in horizontals names departed.
Where else could one find such moving symbols
So displayed for future generations?

Maybe it's the crude obtrusive silence
And the air which makes the place so reverent,
Or perhaps the sighed relief that someone
Else and not yourself is of the future.

In the half-light of the concrete entrance
Which divides the street from what lies hidden,

Can one nullify the passed or passing

Once encountered, really is the present!

1965

Tightrope

Between the cliffs,

The one of granite, the one of lime,

The wire is stretched,

So loose and frailly slender it appears

At breaking point.

Yet there, the weighted balance in his grip

He stands unmoved.

And slowly now he moves across the gap

As wide as life.

About, the hills are still with bated breath;

The hours drag –

Until at last the point of no return:

The point of truth,

Where independence is the final test

And strength the gain,

The juncture of the mountain and the wire

Is reached in sweat.

A journey such as this is never light

Nor is the end,

The means (if borne with faith)

Is what was right!

1965

On the passing of Winston Churchill

The head of this – the world – is bowed,
And grief attends upon its heart;
Nor can we even now depart
From what was then to us endowed.
A man is counted by his deeds,
Not just the thoughts he has;
And though he is no more, alas!
We are the offshoots of his seeds.
But this is not the creed he craved –
A genuflecting human race;
No, rather one defiant face,
And every challenge to be braved.

1965

A New Year Resolution

Another year has just been welcomed in
By those who watched the old one leave;
They watched it and they did not grieve
As if they all perceived their deadly sin
Aware that how the fleeting hours leave
A stillness that is heavy yet so thin.
The air is laden with expectancy
While fear drips slowly from each brow,
They seem like farmers round a plow
Who wait for rain they know will never be.
It's Fate to whom they now must bow
And hope their way of life will never flee.
Away! Remove this burden from my back
While there is time; thank heavens I'm not Black.

1966

Expression

The poem that embraces all –

The empty page.

The drama that reveals the pall –

A silent stage.

As yet unwritten and unsaid –

The life of man.

As vacant, silent as the dead –

The dream of man.

For every day or month or year

That passes by,

Each moment lived is like a tear

We have to dry.

A marble slab, a mound of soil -

The dying knell,

The fateful ending of our toil,

That breaks the spell.

The unfulfilling is the thought

Throughout our life:

Our need to know cannot be taught,

But only learned though strife.

1966

The Painter

Reviving scenes that went by in a rush
He seeks to capture all the passing years;
As image upon image fogs his welling tears;
He reaches out to take his sable brush
To paint and so erase his growing fears
That life is but a momentary kiss.
The oils are mixed to colors deep and true
And placed upon the canvas long-prepared –
An action as of one who now has dared
To paint the thoughts he yet knows to be true:
That childhood is a springtime to be spared
For Summer's ever-draining golden hue.
The Artist and his easel on a Hill –
A print within a picture ever still.

1966

Birth of a first child

The petals blossomed on the rose,
In blushing innocence sublime;
A moment captured so in time
Remains impressed upon the close
Observer of this pantomime
Of Nature in a still repose.
Can any man be witness so
Without the feeling birth is more
Than just a fleeting puppet show;
Or that the comfort of the glow
Of life created is the core
Which men for man can hold in store?
The dream of life exposed is real
That only those aware can feel.

1966

Burning tyres*

Fears abound in men who walk this prison
Barred with eyes and walled with threats of silence;
Where to speak the truth is known as Treason
And remaining silent, acquiescence.

Individuality as Freedom
To express oneself in thoughts and actions
Is suppressed in any failing country;
This alone the price you pay for Safety!

Those who think are labelled Commie bastards,
Those who don't are called unchristian villains;
Those who pray accordingly are 'Ons s'n'.**
Those who don't are grouped as pitied leeches.

No God or State can delegate the freedom
For which people are forever searching;

And when conscience cries out loud in anger

It includes the act of burning tyres!

1966

**In Apartheid-era South Africa placing tyres around people's necks and setting them alight was a popular way of taking vengeance on those they considered to be informers*

Ons'n is an Afrikaans word for 'us' as opposed to 'them'

A little bit of nonsense

There are some of us who do
And some of us who don't'
I could never be like you
For I am one who won't.
There are things we ought to do
And others that we should not;
But I am me and you are you
And some things I just could not.
There are things with ifs and buts
That face us all each day;
But all that I can say is "Nuts!"
I much prefer a good au lait!
There are people who I like
And some I'd rather shun,
There are some I just dislike
Just because they're not much fun! 1966

Zarathustra

There is a time of life in every man
He feels that there are deeds he has to do,
Apply the learning that he knows he knew,
And justify the present living he began.
The action rarely fits intended 'ought's',
And causes panic like a ghost abroad –
A specter of the night that cuts the cord
That joins the base to elevated thoughts.
But Zarathustra lived upon the Mount,
The truth he spread below has been withdrawn –
Intended for the children yet unborn
It lies – a pitcher and an empty fount.
The sands of time have run their grainy course,
And robbed us of his vital one resource.

1966

Chess

The interplay – defending and attack –
Confined to squares of either white or black
Is but a microcosm of the rack
Each player's stretched upon to crack.
The torment felt when silence fills the air,
The anguish of the gambits being foiled;
The pain when prudent planning gets recoiled,
The ache of feeling nothing but despair.

And slowly, slowly, one by one the board
Is cleared and stalemate is the last resort;
If this for which the battle had been fought
Then neither one will gain the last reward.
Two minds in conflict so are caught,
When neither one is willing to abort!

1967

To Artemis

Man has walked upon the moon
Proving dreams are made of rocks:
'One step forward for Mankind!'

Even now it seems insane
Thinking that we're dust to dust,
When we are computerized!
1968

The Nursery

The hyacinths did not reach bloom this year.

They died.

Though some had said the soil would nurture life,

And some that water was just like a tear.

They lied.

I know, I felt the sap upon my knife.

The arum lilies were the only ones to stay.

They wept

Their spathes had heaved like bosoms racked with fear,

And in the twilight looked a little grey.

They slept.

A last resort when no one's there to hear.

The seasons all remained the blankness same.

They're dead.

If only action matched the urge restrained,

There would have been a chance to shout a name.

Unsaid.

But freedom rarely reaches all it's gained.

Perhaps next year the flowers will still grow.

And be.

The seeds are sowed, and time is everywhere.

And in a way we never really know.

To see.

For what was planted once may still be there.

1968

Que será

In this accelerated age of man
The flow of thoughts and visions have increased;
The pace of change so rapid it has squeezed
Us into caves from where we can but scan
The endless battlefield of love and hate,
The shadows moving in the twilight's haze,
Their words and deeds that constantly amaze,
Our memories of our once ancient state.
If this is life, then what is that called death?
If this is no less than a man-made dream
Then nothing is what we would have it seem.
Is death Reality and life its breath?
If what we call a soul is in a gene
Then what will be, will be, because it's been!

1968

Confession

O Self! I do believe that what I knew

About my ego, id, libido too,

Was based on what I wanted them to do,

And so I nurtured them, and so they grew.

But now, in finding that I hardly know

What they evoke in those they act upon,

The certainty I had seems to have gone,

Replaced by no more than a feeble glow.

But all is not replete, nor can it be,

While in me beats the drum that ever calls,

Reminding me that nothing rarely palls

Enough to cloud the vision I can see.

O Self! The time has come for me to act

Upon those parts of you I made a pact! 1968

Gregory

There is a river I will cross someday
And over which I'll carry all my dreams;
But like the threads from which they all were spun
Will stay unravished through the void of time.
All this I know as surely as you are:
My morning and my evening star of love,
The dew that nestles in and feeds the rose;
The rain-washed sky and rainbow's end,
And yes! The first sprung seed I ever sowed.
My heart is full, and tears too deep to flow
Reflect with pool-like lustre all your charms:
Your grey-green eyes, your silver golden hair,
Your limbs as sturdy as an ageless oak;
Your gay abandon and your sense of mirth,
Your spring-like laugher and your smile of joy.
Yet these are pale beside your knitted brow
Behind which lies a dogged search for truth:

The why? The how? The workings of a mind

That speaks of deeds that will in time be wrought

To stand out as a tribute to your soul.

1968

The Dream

I dreamed a dream last night and in it saw
Myself both as the dreamer and the dreamed;
So metaphysic was it that it seemed
I was contained yet free in viewing all
That was occurring and occurred before,
As for the future which I would have deemed
Be unresolved I realised was teamed
With what had been and held me still in thrall.

I saw a coffin as they wound it down,
And as the wood-earth smell became profound
I heard the dulling thuds of spade-flung ground
Already filling up my hollow tomb.
At once I was the knower and the known,
The reason for and keeper of the mound
On which all agonies and hopes compound
To force this hapless dreamer dread his doom.

I see a house where all the clocks stop still
At half-past three the same day every week;
So, like a waking dream it seems I seek
That moment even when it is not here.
The call of Death's appointed time is chill,
For as it pales the pallor of my cheek
I realise the past is so unique
It cannot ever truly disappear.

I woke up from a dream last night today
To find the sun had died and I was cold
With all the loneliness of being old
Before my time, and having no one near
To understand the thoughts-in-words I say.
In moments such as this no dreams are bold
Enough to quell the fear and its strong hold
Around that which the past has made so clear. 1968

Then is now

Death is long time coming – slowly, slowly,
Slowly drooping with the eyelids slowly
Dropping with the tears that keep on falling
Slowly falling with the features falling.

Death is too soon coming – quickly, quickly
With the sudden rush of dying, quickly
Rushing with the pulse that's too soon ebbing
Quickly drains the life-force dammed for ebbing.

Life is long time passing – fading, fading,
Fading with the lengthened shadows fading
Into twilight with its shadows looming
Always growing with that darkness looming.

Life is too soon being – throbbing, throbbing
With excitement measured by the throbbing
No one dares to stop to measure beating

In the panic-pounding heart still beating.

Where we are is there – neither, neither

Neither knowing where we are – neither

Knowing where we will be in a moment

Either now or then is just a moment.

1968

The Final Word

We touched the stars together, you and I
Together in a silent piercing shriek;
We felt the ice-cold shock of outer space
And knew that in it we had by-passed time.
Alone upon a dark and distant shore
We lay exposed to both the wind and sea;
Awareness like the flowing tide grew deep -
So deep, we felt that it could never ebb.
The stars winked out above our naked heads,
And in its wake the light of dawn soon broke;
But still we slept within that waking dream
That shuts out fears of that much longer sleep.
Since then the stolen years have passed me by
Without requesting me to seek regret;
And though I can recall both space and time,
My mind that does so is not what it was.
They say the body seeks its recompense

Within that very moment after death;

Relaxed without a mind to keep control

A man ejaculates without a sigh!

1969

Freedom

There is a world out there, I know, I've been
Beyond my self-reliant body cell
And seen the many different people there;
It seems they know so little of the hell
Of loneliness, that deep and dark despair
That comes from knowing you have not been seen!

There is a world out there, I've heard, I've read
Of men made timid through their fear to act
From love – a fault that shy men oft repeat.
Where circumstances let no man retract
Or veer away from what will be defeat,
So, such a man must live in mortal dread.

There is a world out there. It's hard. It's soft.
It seems that people all embrace their fate
Once freedom is allowed to be expressed.

Such moments rare must surely elevate

The captive soul to fly, where unrepressed

It finds the freedom to remain aloft.

1969

Slow Burn

When in this hurried state of things
We look at what we have achieved,
We pale before the towering cliffs
Of looming heights we still must scale
And dreams we have not yet fulfilled.
No man is worthy of his toil
Who rests content with what he has;
For all too soon he lays to waste
The deep foundations he has sunk
To build the structures of his life.
Perhaps our lives are all the same
In fashioning the dreams we dream,
And not unlike ancestral man
Confronted by his daily fears
Retires to a cave to cringe. 1969

Final awareness

Can one recall the splendors of the past,
And unify them all to see them now;
Can one erase the wrinkles on my brow,
And smooth them out in such a way they last?
Now more than ever must I face the fact
That life is one short footpath to the grave;
And there is nothing I can do to save
Me from the truth no matter how I act.
Through this short life but once will I pass through,
Nor will I ever know the reason why;
Yet at the very moment that I die
Still everyone will tell you that I knew.
And through their hearts will flow a common theme:
That all of this was not an empty dream.

1969

The river

A river of people surged and passed me by
On either side, but I alone was there;
They came from tributaries everywhere,
Uncaring, so it seemed, if they would die.
And so, it is, at times, when all alone
I see myself an island in a sea
Detached from all this life surrounding me,
Yet knowing I could never wear like stone.
To die within the living world is real;
Nor is it just a wild abstracted thought;
For only while I breathe can I still feel
What pain is, death is not so clearly wrought.
If I should stay unmoved by this great Flood,
Then let me join the river with my blood.

1969

To be is not to be

You can count the years in footfalls
As they measure out your time,
And with each receding echo
Know which doors to shut behind.
There is only this long passage
Lined with fear on either side;
But you cannot see the ending
As the darkness makes you blind.
Bring back the past through all your dreaming
It is all that you can own –
All the faces that are in it
Are for you and you alone.
You can feel your pace has altered
When you have to pause to sigh,
And with each receding echo
Count the doors you shut behind.
O how wearily youth suffers

When it comes to realise

That with every passing moment

All the time it got has gone.

1969

Bust out!

Bust out!

People remind me of time,

Beauty of all that must pass,

Nature of all that will be;

Knowledge reminds me of love!

How is a waterfall made;

Why is a sunset so red;

When was the first scent of Spring,

How can such love be recalled?

Bust out!

Life is a permanent change,

Love is impermanent, too;

Knowledge revealed is the Path!

Bust out!

1970

This age

There is music in the wind
Of the early morning air
Blowing soft against my cheek.

Like the laughter children make
Adults wake too late to know
Is the sound the heavens hear.

1970

Surmising

Sunlight sifting through the sable trees
Turns the stream into a silver spool
Sleeving as it trickles to the pool,
Silent in its ageless reveries.
Time does not impede its common course,
Nature in its basic form is mute;
Only man is altered by the brute
He himself has wakened at its source.
We can draw some comfort from these facts
Knowing we are moving with the stream,
That we too will also have the dream
When we pass beyond the cataracts.
Until then we'll pass through light and shade
Sure our common senses never fade.

1971

The Storm

You can see the spider's web:

Lightning in electric white

On the black clouds of a storm.

Hypnotised by fear (or hope?)

You are drawn to what seems right;

Yet you go – a fly at heart!

1971

Gd is four years' young*

When my son asked me

"Where is God?"

I had to tell him

"Everywhere."

When my son asked me

"Does God have legs?"

I had to tell him

"He cannot walk."

When my son asked me

"Does God have a head?"

I had to tell him,

"God is in your head."

When my son asked me

"Is God in *your* head?"

I had to tell him

"Yes, he's in my head."

What will I tell my son

When he asks again?

I'll have to whisper

"You know, because you asked."

1971

*Based on a dialogue involving the words herein actually used between my son, Gregory, and me last night. 17th January 1971.

Third party insurance

a man is made immortal through his child;
And through the DNA he passes on
Ensures the future links up with the past.

But here no safe insurance can be bought
That children will not fly upon the wind
And leave their parents trapped within their dreams.

For all too late a man must be aware
He stands alone beneath a million stars
Where only calm can help him ease the shock.
1971

Rebirth

After seven years a shoot

opened on my rubber plant

Green with promise and with hope.

Looks like time will hold back life

Waiting for that final breath

Needed to fulfil a dream.

1971

The prison of the mind

'Stone walls do not a prison make

Nor iron bars a cage' (Lovelace)

Looking at the Wailing Wall

I can taste the dust of time

Mixing with my falling tears.

Like a dying lover's thoughts

Making all that was more real

Than the present he can feel.

1971

Milestone 31

I see my memories arise before
me like the ghosts of half-forgotten dreams
that haunt me with recurrent chilling themes
to make me cower on a distant shore.
And they will come, I know, forevermore
unless my faith is stronger than it seems.
Some say I should effect a compromise
and others that I am a dream-filled fool;
And both that thought is more than just tool
to fashion what the heart and soul devise.
And yet … and yet... the sages who advise
are those whose streams have dammed the sacred Pool.
To die is simple - life is more profound
and must be lived for every moment known,
for every cloud on which a thought has flown
and every act performed upon the ground;
Indeed, in all, before they heap the mound

no life was lived if it was lived alone.

1971

Oil Crisis

This world has been put

Over a barrel

Of a gun, and oil.

There is no escape.

Be content with now!

1971

The gift

Give a child a dreamed-of toy,

And the now and then will blend

For as long as time allows.

All too soon we're dispossessed,

And the wanting as is had

All too soon becomes our dread!

1971

Gregory (2)

No moment could have been quite so sublime
As when you raised your hand towards your nose
And drank in deep the scent of one white rose
Fresh cut and soft as nature in its prime.
'It smells so sweet,' you said in perfect time,
'That I should like to eat it.' Such repose
As I saw in your eyes just then, no prose
Could dare express it, even measured rhyme.
A five years' world is recognising love,
Not knowing that in time it soon will fade
No matter how the game of life is played.
How then can we as adults look above
And not draw comfort when they wonder why
The rose's scent is redolent of love?

1971

Wrong way

Someone turned a signpost round

Making all the traffic flow

On the wrong side of the road.

Like the victims of a hoax

We have all been taught to go

Counter to our inner flow.

1971

Fireplace

Ice blue flames on red hot coals
Shiver as they lose their heat
In the slowly cooling grate.

So affections soon expire
When the glowing passions chill
On a cold, unloving bed,

1971

Reality

There is a fear-grey time before the dawn,
When chill uncertainty assails the soul
About to stir from that deep-caverned sleep
Which seals man off from time's unfeeling beat.
There is a breathless hush before a birth,
When tender trepidation grips the heart
About to throb alone within that breast
Which bares man open to his capsuled space.
There is an ecstasy before a death,
When falling fear embraces dying dreams
About to shatter from that fragile cloud
Which shields a man from what is real or not.
There is a man who sees life in the round:
This writer, who can dream and live, at once.

1971

Bus queue, Johannesburg

Every night at six o'clock

I can see the lines of black

Etched against the smoglit sky.

Like the canvas of their lives

Stretched to anonymity

By the force of other hands.

1971

Apathetic

Walking through a crowded face
I can feel its melting mask
As its features separate.

Man has lost his jungle soul,
When to flee or fight was all;
Now he simply walks away!
1971

Vision

There was a time when I believed my dream
Believed my dream would soon be realised,
Would soon be more than what it symbolized,
Be more than what I would have had it seem.
I would I had it not just as a dream
That keeps recurring cold and undisguised,
Repeating rather what was in the scheme
Was what I knew I could have improvised.
The leaves have turned from green to yellow white,
The sky from blue to clouded shades of fear;
Like all of summer blended in a tear
I will not be allowed to shed at night.
If all of this seems less than what I dreamed
Perhaps in truth I will have been redeemed.

1972

Black September

At this year's Olympic Games
Every starter's gun was raised
Even though their deaths were known.

I am saddened at the thought
Men had little more to gain
Than the price upon their heads.

In one hundred years from now
No one will know or recall why
This September, Gd had died.
1972

I am that I am

Through the endless night of my fear,
Shadows come and go. Silently.
Figureless forms that seem to be
Moving away yet drawing near.
In this timeless state I can feel
Myself together with a past
That has yet to be, but cannot,
For the present lies in between.
All that is of now is living –
That awareness there is nothing
Quite as unacceptable as
Time that has a certain ending!
Knowing that I know I can think
I know what I think is what I am.

1972

Hell is people (Sartre)

In a mirror that is cracked
Neither face is quite the same
When a shadow falls on one.

Such dichotomy must be
When a cause and its effect
Are disjoined by one false word!

1972

The fact is this….

It is a bare land.

There are no shadows

Where the sun burns black.

There are only shacks

Sweaty with the heat

Of rusted iron.

An endless sweetlush sea of rippling green

Flows back and forth between the purple hills

Between which pools from icy mountain rills

Remain concealed behind the high tree screen.

It is a dry land.

There are little rains

Where the corn husks crack;

You can hear the fowls

Pecking at the sand

Between the wire strands.

But wait! Ms. I-beg-your-pardon-who
Beneath her insulated drying hood,
With magazines of glacéd instant food
Is quite perturbed at what she's going to do!

It is a far land.
No ships pass through it.
Where the railhead ends
There is only veld
And the sound of drums
At birth, marriage, death.

Below in caves and high on mountain plains
There are, I've read, some modern secret sites
Where signaling and early warning lights
Protect us day and night from red-starred planes.

It is an old land.
The fossils prove it.
Where the sites remain
Tourists see their birth

As the well-trained guides

Remind them it's their death.

And yet this country is so very new

We have been told by those who claim to know!

"In nineteen-forty-eight there was no snow"

And who will argue now that that's untrue!

1972

Fragility

I can feel the brittle crunch

Of the dead leaves as I walk

Over Summer's fallen face.

Dreams are just as delicate

When constructed in the hope

What you wish for will come true.

1972

Ode to man

The broken earth exhaled its dust-dry air
As spade-heaped clods exploded on its chest;
His folded pair of arms survived the test
His eulogy became a loud affair.

It matters not whose fate is sealed with earth:
For some it shuts out what it is to be,
For others it permits no memory
To cloud the freedom of a newfound birth!

And inasmuch as life and death conceal
The pathways that are safe to walk,
They reaffirm that dead men cannot talk
And those alive dare not unless they shout.

No single act confers more freedom gained
Than what we think's the passing of a man;

Nor is there more than what's revealed than
Than just how far our lives are unrestrained!

Since Eve first tempted Adam into sin,
All men have been betrayed by love;
Not that sublime affection from above,
But that irreverent passion from within!

No man has ever felt the pain of birth
That only women know is felt by them;
The agony of man is in his stem
Forever measured by its joyous girth!

If what I have described seems quite absurd –
Then note how all the men in pine-wood coats
Are now no more than anecdotes
Whose deeper meanings now are somewhat blurred.

1972

Munich, 1972

When eleven men were killed -

Shot by non-competing foes

Everyone just groaned with shock.``

But it was an inconvenience –

Grateful grief had no effect.

The Olympic Games went on.

1972

Sunset

I have seen the sun go down,

Taking with it all the warmth

Of a summer's afternoon.

In the twilight of our lives

We will try to count the stars,

Doubting whether we were here!

1973

Ruff my dog

I can’t see you anymore
With your head upon the sill
Waiting for me to caress.

You can't see me anymore
Yet your yelp and cry will live
Deep-remembered in my mind.

There is nothing quite as pure
As the single-minded love
Of a trusting dog and man.

As of now I hear your howl
Wanting to return to life
And to be as one again.

Would the tears I shed be blood

Surging life into your heart,

I would never cease. I won't?

1973

Cause and effect

Have you ever seen a stone
being thrown into a pool
and the way the ripples spread?

Like the liquid of my life
which is moved by every beat,
I am not insensitive to words.
1973

Let there be light

Suddenly a darkened cloud

Came between the sun and me

And I felt alone. And cold.

Warmth is vital to exist;

Like the light upon your skin

And the glow within your thoughts.

1973

Karate

I come to you with open hands -
These hands that can both love and kill;
For such is that most artful skill
A man of freedom understands.
For what is man if he is bound
By uncontrolled emotions, or
The mind that knows no reason for
The voice that speaks without a sound!
I bare my being by my acts,
Nor would I wish it otherwise,
For that would be to shut my eyes
And so pretend there were no facts.
For that is why I am not shy
When I embrace - or shout, 'Kiai!'

1973

For what do we grieve?

On the self- same tree, I've seen

Leaves that died before the rest;

Some quite high and some quite low.

Life has no set hierarchy,

Nor has time a fixed resolve.

Only death outlives its course!

1973

Interlude

I have known the warmth of love
And the chill of loneliness.
There is nothing in between!

Peace is nothing but a pause
In the permanence of war.
All the precedents are there!

1973

Tree of life

I have seen a fruit-ripe tree
Standing utterly unmoved
Wrapped in nothing but its leaves.

Clothed in doubt a dreamer dreams;
Don't! Then always wonders if…
Do! Then then always wonders why?
1973

Love lost

Was all of this by Fate ordained,
A Grand Design or self-conceived?
Was there a splendid masterplan
On which I was a simple sketch
That does not show or verify
Some revelation of the fact
My pain is real, and all the more
Severe because no echo's heard –
No sound to separate my voice
That cries aloud in silent grief
Within the caverns of my mind?
For what, I ask, was all this for?
A word, a look, a touch of love
That's all. It's all there was. I know!

1974

Flight of fancy

When looking up I gazed upon the sea
And saw the birds that that sail upon its foam;
I saw their outstretched wings caress the dome
With gentle strokes in silent harmony.
At once my thoughts were hurled to roam
In search for something in that symphony.
Imagination flies when faced with dull
Monotony or chains around its feet;
But most of all when that responsive beat
Becomes a muffled echo in my skull.
I wonder who is more the freedom bird -
The one who flies much higher than the rest,
The one who gathers feathers for the nest,
The one who walks like me - now that's absurd!

1974

New Year 1975

They were signing 'Auld Lang Syne'
As the old year, wreathed in mist
Flowed down Table Mountains' side.

Like the future I must find,
Like the past I left behind
Underneath a life-swept rock.

1975

Hluhluwe

I have listened to the veld
Hearing nothing but my thoughts
Muted by the whispering air.

Would my mind were so at peace,
And as silent as the hills,
I would gladly welcome life.

1975

Atom bomb

I am a bomb,

With a severed umbilicus

Triggered at birth

To self-destruct,

Anywhere…anytime.

Ticking seconds

Measured by my beating heart:

Built-in safety –

I will not explode,

Just implode

To fragmented dust.

Will there be sound?

Maybe just a whimper –

Not a bang!

1975

South Africa 1975

Panic clutches at my gut,
Leaving solid emptiness
And a feeling of despair.

One thing's certain – and it's death;
It's the unrest of the time
That creates uncertainty.

1975

Truth

There was a time when every word and deed
Was meant to cover up my deepest thoughts
Through every letter which I wrote in verse
Or uttered face to face to those I knew.
That time has gone – there is no need to lie –
For truth, as always, is a fact of life.
For so it was that every wisp of cloud
And crimson sunset blanketed my soul
Beneath a mountain full of metaphors
To hide the feelings I could not express.
That time has gone – the figures of my speech -
Now they no longer soothe my hell bound soul,
Or slow the heavy drumbeat of my heart.
The rest of what I live is plain to see.

1975

Call of the sea

The bubbling breakers bursting on the beach
Reveal the tide that flows – the melody –
Or hide the tide that ebbs – the threnody –
The one that seems so often out of reach.
The pleading sounds of seagulls also call
To long-forgotten memories that rest
Behind the muffled time-beat in my breast,
And which, try as I might, I can't recall.
Could I but stem the tides a little while
And see the shadowline in clear relief,
I might be able to arrest my grief
So easily disguised behind my smile!
So long as man is mastered by the sea
We can but hope the future's meant to be.

1975

Ah! Sweet mystery of love

Have you ever filled one spoon,

Poured a measure in a cup,

Realised you've had your share?

Like the granules in a bowl,

Sweetness is a preplanned dose;

When you've had your share, that's all!

1975

Autumn sunset

Red and gold, the oak-trees' leaves
Whisper dryly in the breeze:
'Summer's spent – the season's fled.'

Like the passing of the years,
When the summer's gone and dusk
Casts a melancholic light.

1975

Suddenly!

Wide across the sky a star came flaring
Out its brilliance, burst, and then it vanished
From my view as if it had been banished
For an indiscretion that was daring.
Or a universal error glaring
In its bright obscenity which ravished
All the mystery it had been lavished
In a timeless, spaceless womb of caring.

Nowhere is the flash of inspiration
Quite so clear as when, without a warning
It appears as suddenly as morning
Snatches at the night in desperation.
Such is dreaming man's imagination:
Only after darkness is there dawning!

1975

Viewpoint

Standing at tomorrow's edge,

I can see the mountain tops

Stretching to a distant haze.

Fixed in time and yet unreached,

All the future rests in now,

And which only dreamers see!

1975

The tortoise and the hare

Have you seen a tortoise crawl,

Measuring its every move

With its life upon its back?

So unlike the frantic man

Deftly changing every course

As he tries to shrug off death!

1976

The unequivocal word

Gently squeezed or finger forced,
When the trigger has been pulled
Nothing can retrieve the shot.

Like the impact of a word
Said without considered thought
Blows the target off its pegs.

1976

Reductio ad absurdum

Yesterday an act of fraud
Was committed by a man;
Someone called it ‘business sense.’

Yesterday a man retired
Though he was only thirty-five;
Some said, ‘his horse came in.’

Yesterday a hijacked plane
Gave a gang a chance to flee:
Someone said, ‘the price was low.’

Yesterday a church was bombed
By a wild and Irish man;
Someone said, ‘Now let us pray.’

Yesterday is like today,

Nothing seems to change it seems;

Of tomorrow? Who can say?

All my life is here and now,

Passing by with every hour;

So I said, ‘Don’t wind the clock!’

1976

Say that again!

What is life if not the truth
That the mind employs the heart
Willing it to stay alive?

What is love if not the truth
That the heart employs the mind
Bidding it to live with hope!

What is life if not the truth
That there is this paradox:
Who's the ruler who the ruled!
1976

In camera

Peering through the lens I see

What will be a memory.

All is have to do is 'click'.

Like a secret wink it seems,

Made so only I can see

My reality is fixed!

1976

Across the Lethe

Sunk within a sea of pain

I encountered depths of fear

My awareness could not check.

Like so many dreams it seems

When you feel there's no escape;

Only dawn brings some relief.

1976

Lines: On Not writing

Empty pages lost in thought
Wonder why the pen that poised
Vanished to this little point.

Pain is like a shattered sky
Uncontrolled and far too high
For my tiny mind to hold!

1976

Johannesburg 1976

A cloud of Black and White arose, then spread
Fear-blown across the whole Witwatersrand.
A single spark had set ablaze the land
And made its dreams as vacant as the dead.

On stone-strewn streets of sand there is no dust
Trod hard by calloused feet and weighted load.
The way to go was not upon this road,
But through the veld abundant with distrust.

From there the ammunition came to hand
For earth to bring to earth the fired clay
In fear-directed anger everyway
Except the cause they did not understand.

No bullet ever was designed to choose
Nor fear to separate the good from bad;

No shell-proof dustbin lid was ever had

Nor fear to ward off madness so let loose.

The fevered days and nights are now less hot,

But winter ills recur – that is our fate,

And if not now, then on another date

Perhaps, perhaps this writer will be shot!

1976

Desert

There is nothing to be seen

In the wasteland of this life –

Nothing but the aftermath.

Like the total loneliness

And the feeling of despair

Of a man who lacks all hope.

1976

Which way?

Clouds are restless, see them drift,
Subject to the thermal flow
And the jet stream in their paths.

Like a man with broken threads
On the spiderweb of life
Does not know which way to go.

1977

Point of no return

There is a point of no return
Beyond which men ought not to go
Or else they die;
If not by some external force
Then by their own hand turning in
Within their mind

There is a moment when the cause
No longer leads to some effect.
It is itself -
Becoming all yet incomplete,
Like unripe fruit just newly plucked,
Beyond itself.

There is a time beyond all time
When life is measureless to Man.
I am what was.

The insignificance of words

Recalls what even Death accepts:

To feel is all!

1977

Wonderworld

The Wonderworld of children is the Dream
That sages have so desperately sought,
But how could they when Ignorance is thought
To be the opposite of Wisdom's scheme.

A Trustingworld where everything is *such*,
And what cannot be understood is dead;
Where god – the spoken word – is in your head
And fear's dispelled by finding out by touch.

A Wakefelt world where dew upon the grass
Leaves footprints only sunbeams can erase;
Where time is unimportant, out of phase,
And what will be has surely come to pass.

A Smilefilled world where tears are quickly dried
Because there is no time to waste 'to do';
Where love reciprocates from one to two,

And where you sleep is where you will abide.

An Answerworld where there must be replies –
No question asked dare have a bar1
Where words mean no more than what they really are
And if, perchance, they do, are surely lies.

The Wonderworld of children is the fact
Of life we seem, or wish, to overlook;
And yet it is the only open book
We all can read and share without a pact!
1977

The circle turns

No year before has been like this,
With months torn out like this and days like that;
A year of loss.
A twelvemonth disappearing face,
And in its place the hooded Reaper stands
A year to gain.

A downtrod generations waits,
As children reach their adulthood in days,
And think of life.
Another, fed on piety,
Sees children fighting for their coloured skin,
And thinks of death.

This land of sunshine now has clouds
As black as doom as any can design
To end the Drought.

The never-ending summer's gone -

Outshone itself by showing off too much

To start the Flood.

And where will we with conscience be

When we set free our tiny tethered minds?

Upon the line.

Returned upon the settlers' way

It seems we may retrace our fathers' dreams.

The circle turns.

1977

Ode to David

Midnight was her shade of hair

Dawn the bloom upon her cheeks,

Dusk the softness of her eyes

Noon the passion in her soul.

Rain her every fallen tear,

Storms the tearing of her grief,

Breezes all her whispered words,

Skies her purity of heart.

Now her seasons have raced by

Dulled by every passing day,

Clouding every probing thought

Trying hard to understand.

Could she have but one wish more,

It's that David was not dead.

1977

Tomb with a view

Sheathed in mist the trees recede
Down just one side of the turf;
It's an uncompleted sketch.

Like the outlook from my grave
Viewed through one unmoving eye,
And I stare at it. Alone!

1977

Spine

Have you heard the crunching sound

Of a dog devouring bones

Grinding them to pointless pulp?

Such was my consuming pain

As my back was shaved to fix

My abrading splinting spine.

1977

Freedom is a word

The "Court of Justice" gathered in its robes –
A silent line of swordsmen cloaked in black;
Was not for them the arms of bold attack
Instead the facts denied to one who probes.
In facing death no man can claim the right
To live another life or even dare
To even ask for anyone to care
What words are uttered at the hanging sight!
I abnegate all rights I had presumed
For they were surely never meant for me!
The irony is that they'll fall to he
Who follows in the path I had assumed.
The final walkway will be bare and cold
And the fateful sentence every old!

1977

Disneyland

When I went to Disneyland

Nearly everyone I saw

Had a twinkle in their eye.

Holding on to youth long gone

Seems a need to be fulfilled,

Or retreating from this life!

1977

Spiderweb

Watch a spider in his web

As he spins to fix the breaks

In his fragile universe.

Unlike man with broken links

On his spiderweb of life

Does not know which way to turn!

1977

Live!

The Act of Being is to be.
Definitively stated, it
Must be complete.
Unless the 'me' accepts the 'we',
There is no way this life can fit,
And be replete.

The world is filled with aching hearts,
All searching for the Golden Thread –
The Loving Fact.
The truth is joining all the parts
Apart is not through thought, instead
Is in the Act.

So like a river is the Way,
And we the islands in its thrust
Must wash away.

Now there can be no holding back,

The mandate given is a Must

To live each day!

1977

Night happens

The sun came sliding
Down the silent trees
Washing darkness from my eyes.

Love-red roses grow
At my garden's edge.
Pain is at my fingertips.

Stars spill out my hands
When I spread my arms
And embrace the universe.

1977

Perhaps...

Perhaps, perhaps a child would cry

If say I had to die today;

Tomorrow is like yesterday

The breath that comes before a sigh.

The shadowline is two feet wide

Between the living and the dead;

And so it is, with measured tread,

That no one wants to step aside.

The unrelenting weight of time

Bears down upon my human frame;

The anguish stays, and is the same

When railed against or said in mime.

There is no sanity to life:

The madness of it ends with death.

1978

The commuter

In the London Underground

People hang on by the straps

Dangling from the roof above.

We are life commuters, all;

Trapped within our artifacts

We hang on to our roots!

1978

Understanding

All my books in neat array

Silently attest a truth:

Men find immortality

When their dreams convert to print.

Should they hide behind their words,

They will die; they must be read!

1978

The Common

Wading through a sea of leaves

I could hear the dripping drops

Falling like so many tears.

Autumn is a sad time, Brown

As the fading skin of man

Just before he turns death white.

1978

Soweto drumbeat

Soweto is a drumbeat from the kraal
A wheel-beat from the town, and in between
A military tattoo that every Queen*
Can hear upon the floorboards in her saal.**
Soweto's feet move like a trembling brush
Across the high hats sounding far and near;
The drum-hard earth now shudders with the fear
That builds before that fright-filled cymbals' rush.
Soweto's voice is as the rising notes
Of trumpets, horns and ardent clarinets;
And all below a screen of cigarettes
Obscuring guns and knives in overcoats.
Soweto is a famous band whose drawl
And music is the beat of life to all.

1978

- Queen. Owner of a beer hall

- ** Saal. A beer hall

Summer madness

I feel detached
And unattached;
At once removed
Yet deeply moved.
I cannot fly
Yet bound to die;
A fact described
A tomb inscribed.
For all alone,
A living clone.
A single breath
Away from death,
I feel confined
Within my mind.
There is no love
Below, above,
And so deprived
I am arrived.

1978

Second-hand man

We trade in what we have for something more
And which, in turn, we trade in once again.
The fact remains we have to be insane
To think the future is an endless store.
Acquiring nothing but a changing rate,
We measure life by what we hope will be
Of higher value at some future fee,
Discounting it against its actual state.
We all are traded in – we're second hand,
Or else we'd live within the present tense,
We'd use the verb 'to be' in every sense,
And keep the minute-timer filled with sand.
How true is Man to his own synonym
When he can say that what is his, is him!

1978

The African Buffalo

(For my son Trevor)

With lowered head he stood alone beneath the trees,
His dark grey bulk dissolved into the shade;
Just two black eyes stared out across the glade
To where I sat, my face against the breeze.

The two-tone buffalo is tough. He smells,
His horns can tear apart a lion's face;
And like a locomotive full of pace
His charge will shrug aside a hail of shells.

No animal quite causes so much fear,
And big game hunters know this best of all:
They know the first shot has to make him fall
Or else they can be sure their death is near.

These thoughts that filled my head have made me sway

As the tall and wind-blown conifers;

For I was looking through binoculars

And was at least a hundred yards away.

Whew!

1978

To Cedric of Guest

I grieve for you

My dog,

Who does not understand,

For in my leaving you

My dog,

I'm losing my best friend.

For thirteen years

My dog,

We shared a common bond

You did not have to speak

For all your moods were mine.

This eulogy

My dog,

Was writ with pain-racked tears;

Deserving death in time

My dog,

Was what you should have had.

The Fates are cruel

My dog,

And I am only man;

Were that our roles reversed

My dog,

I'd give my life for yours

Ave!

My dog,

Your memory is mine!

1978

To my sons

To pick you up and hold you in my arms,
To climb a tree or tumble on the grass,
To kick a ball and show you how to pass,
To teach you skills to harbor you from harms.
To do for you the things I wish I could
Is gone, yet I would wish it were not so;
But all-embracing pain is all I know
And my too-fragile frame is hollowed wood.
I would I could explain my angst to you,
And so be pardoned for my embered fire,
For there is nothing more I would desire
Than to be the fatherman you know you knew.
I fear my grip on life is easing fast
And all too soon will fade into the past.

1978

On: My landing

It is a cold land.
Beneath the soft snow
Black ice forms a crust.
Birds can find no food.

I wander through uncertainties
Surrounded by a shield of metaphors.
To let my fears assert themselves
Would bind me to a three- word epitaph.

It is a sacred land.
No one wants to lose;
No one wants to win.
Indecision reigns

I rest my weary feet in dreams
Allowing them to give me sustenance.

Embracing life's realities

Would leave me with no clear identity.

It is a wet land.

Water on a sponge

Drains away when pressed,

But not so with clay.

I hammer at the door of love

For understanding to allow me in.

To let my dreams dictate my moves

Is all I have to get me through this time.

1979

Five Seasons

Winter in an overcoat
Stepped across the City's feet,
Leaving footprints made of ice
On the black unyielding street.
Summer in a sultry mood
Drooped one eyelid slowly down
Leaving tearstains on the clouds
Wrapped around the moon's wan cheeks.
Autumn hiding in the shade
Played with mounds of leaves of gold,
Capturing awhile the feel
Of a fading currency.
Springtime in a fresh-face look
Fluttered lashes at the buds
Leaving hearts with skipping beats
Breathlessly awaiting love.
Death, forever, in disguise,

Crushes seasons every way -

Plain or simple it is not;

Who else can dictate its terms!

1979

One-way ticket

The fear of life – that body punch
Which hits you unexpectedly –
Is fearing death.
Awake there is no other thought,
Asleep there is no other fact
Which can be killed.

The fear of death is knowing that;
And knowing after death that that
Is all there is.
Nor will there be or can there be
Between the moment now and then
A break in time.

There is no getting out of this,
The one-way, paid-for-ticket ride
We didn't want.

We are not given any choice

Within the womb, or else we'd know

It was our tomb.

1979

Queendom

The honey badger kills its prey
By biting off its balls;
Emasculation cuts off life.
The female praying mantis eats
its mate directly after sex.
The sexual act decapitates!
Secretions from the Queen ant tells
each subject what it must perform;
The mind controlled is mind content.
The Queendom of the animals
is predicated on the male
accepting he is second-hand.
And those who dare and do rebel
become the wonders of the zoos!

1979

Israel-Egypt Peace Treaty

The heavens wept
the night they signed
their lands away.

As such, can man
recall the tears
he shed in joy?
1979

Because

I am

as tense

as the imperative!

Existence has

no point

past the end of this sentence.

Reality

is the pluperfect –

and the future

the subjunctive.

Playing with words

is not to be articulate

but literate!

So composed –

I conjugate my feelings

decline my ears

and wonder if you've read this far

you know

what I really meant!

1979

Burial

In the falling shadows
hear their voices murmur,
listen to their prayers
end in solemn amens.
People lose their features
long before they're buried
in the shattered sunlight
underneath the cypress.
It's the earth that nurtures
everything upon it,
Keeping time in measures
By its turning hours.
1979

Jerusalem

O Jerusalem, your stone is white;

Whiter than your sun-bleached fossil bones,

Whiter than the salt of dried out tears,

Whiter than the clouds that bring no rain.

O Jerusalem, who bow to you,

Wish for peace to those who plead to you,

For the wisdom Solomon was known

No one now seems able to discern.

1979

Beachcomber

The seagull's cry is whipped
away by the winds he fights.
Becalmed, he struts and frets
and walks the shores alone.
His independence is
the being of his life –
depending on his food
he either lives or dies.
How wide his wings extend
dictates the world he knows;
and so described reveals
he is not bound to seas!
One thing he does not fear
and that is man – the man
who shares his solitude,
and cries into the wind.   1979

Jerusalem (2)

There's a permanence about the place

Knowing if you stay you'll never die.

You can feel it in the timebleached stones

And the bones the earth surrenders up.

Face to face with who we really are

We can only contemplate our fate.

1979

Shame!

They say they fall from open windows. Shame!
They say such actions are the deeds of fools
Who lost their senses and are mindless tools
Employed by people whom they cannot name.

They say the Children have no values. Shame!
They say that throwing stones is dangerous,
That burning schools is treacherous.
So shoot them! Caning, as you know, is tame!

They say some people want their freedom. Shame!
They say that only Calvinists believe
In one true God whose minions will relieve
Oppression by possession of their Claim.

They say the future is not black. Oh Shame!
And censorship is for the common good,

And that is why there is the Brotherhood.

And they are right. That's why I have no name!

1978

Quo Vadis?

It is a changing time –
A time of standing still,
A time of knowing nothing will
Or could be as it was;
There is so little time.
Effect does have a cause!

No age was ever so –
An age that has no face,
An age that cannot stay in place.
Advancing in retreat
It goes where people go,
And still is lost in space.

It is land of dreams,
Of dreams that are not real,
Of dreams that all too soon reveal

Reality is bare.
For what you touch, it seems
You could, but do not dare.

This life is all there is,
A life which living kills,
A life where every moment fills
A man with love or fear;
Or prove that grieving is
The essence of a tear!
1978

Butterflies are free

Pinning butterflies on boards

Captures beauty in its blush.

If you wish to get the point –

Even death can have appeal.

Such vicarious deceit

Is the folly of our kind –

Only those who are so free

Keep their immortality!

Think of words as butterflies

Captured by the pinpoint pen!

Only so can beauty stay

As the concept and the deed.

Writing, therefore, guarantees

That words once penned are pinned.

1978

Mandela

The winds that blow cross the mine-dumps leave
A veil of dust apparent only when
You wipe your finger on the sill; it's then
You know no matter what you trace or weave
The truth is not what you alone believe,
But what is real to ordinary men.
There is no wind within a sightless cell.
No dust to outline islands in the sky;
For here all dreams are broken lie by lie
And given to the media to sell
As facts that only 'honest' men would tell;
And if you don't believe them you could die!
It's white by night and black by day out there,
From here Mandela's dream is everywhere!

1978

Time is

In the fullness of time,

there is no time.

Time is a face you watch,

It's a dream you dread

It's a deadline someone set.

Changing dates on a stone

Doesn't alter your time.

Made in God's image,

I am that I am -

a figment of His imagination.

How can we own

What is not ours?

How can we be in time

When we're not here in space!

1980

Death is indifferent

Death is indifferent,

Life is the difference

Between the not knowing

And what we think we know.

Death could not care less.

Life is about caring

And all about loving

Whoever fills our hearts,

Whatever fills our thoughts.

1980

Tel Aviv

As the sun sets on the sea,

People walking on the shore

Are like cardboard silhouettes.

There's a spotlight on our lives

Showing who we really are:

Targets in a gallery!

1980

Nuweiba

A first no more than just a probing light
Appeared beyond the dark and distant dunes;
And then as swiftly as the rush of dawn
Its brilliance grew so bright the stars were dimmed.
I see it now – it was the rising moon
Which now had cast its earthlight on the sea.

Across the waters where I stood in awe
I saw it sidling slowly up the sky -
A satellite observing alien life
In that dark region where the world is split
Between opposing forces old as men
Aware that each of them is being watched.

How strange these waters should appear so still
And unaffected by the lunar spell
That's cast on other seas around the world;

Deep waters such as these perhaps await

That moment when the moon becomes transfixed

And all opposing forces find their peace.

1980

To Brian

The spells you cast with words construed
Will sentence you to write, and so
Reveal the feelings that you know
Are real and can be understood.

As words are tools to fashions dreams,
So must you learn to master them;
In doing so you'll find a gem
Is made more precious when it gleams.

1980

Canvas

I remember how I walked
Over leafwet pavements as
Coldwet winds and treelow clouds
Shrouded all the greendamp trees?

Underneath the winter's cold
Dragging down my every step
I implored with sagging hope
Sunlight soon would reappear.

London is a memory
That is harder now to paint
On my canvas rich and rare,
Dry as drought and splashed in light,
Forms the background blue and bright

To the landscape I just drew.

1981

Foghorn

Have you ever heard the sound
Of a foghorn out at sea
Waiting for the tugboat's call?

Like a plaintive note it seems
Of a muted minstrel's pipe
Played in hope for love to hear.
1981

Insomnia

In a single leap
To hear that distant call;
Thinking what I'll do
Tomorrow not today.

Love as I once knew
Is buried in my brain –
Unexpressed in time,
Unexplored in space.

Time has lost its thread,
So all that matters now
Is the filling up
Of gaps between each sleep.

Trembling on the brink

Of these uncertainties,

I am dead awake

Yet cannot fall asleep.

1981

To: My sons

Think about this moment. Now.
In a flash it is the past
And tomorrow? It's a dream.

So, my children, growing up,
Know reality is what
You commit to memory!
1983

Interferon Dream

I used to dream
Of lots of things
I'd do someday.

Now I don't dream.
It's hard to live
From day to day.

To measure life
In finite terms
Is second hand.

1985

Treatment break

I was three years old again today
Ankle deep and standing in the surf
As the waves came breaking down on me.

I saw myself that little boy again,
Felt at once the selfsame awe and fear
In the presence of a greater force.

1985

Balance

Balancing on a tightrope
Above a sea of faces -
It's the greatest show on earth!

Just how long we each survive
Depends upon our balance,
And not fearing we will fall.

1985

Time

I'm running out of time
To do the things I must;
I'm running out of time
Before I turn to dust.
There's much that must be done
Before the day has flown;
I'm not the only one
Who knows what will be known.
The time for dreaming's gone,
There's very little hope;
And yet I'm not alone
I have His hand to cope.
I'm running out of time
To make my world sublime.

1986

Thoughts on dying

In limbo,

a time of waiting,

waiting, waiting.

Somewhere

between now and then.

All alone

except for the One,

and I'm not ready

to take that step

until He says so.

Somehow

I just thought

it would be different.

Maybe it still will be!

1986

Timeless

Have you watched the sun go down

At the ending of the day

Knowing it will rise again?

Is there anything more sure –

Death has no finality

On the universal wheel.

1987

Swan song

Every man condemned to die
Is permitted one last wish,
One last free and conscious act.
Face to face with death reveals
We all really have one choice -
Until death we have to live!
There's so little left of time,
There's no scale to weigh the odds,
Or defer what should be done.
Taking one last fling at life
Reaching for His guiding hand,
Praying G-d will ease the way.
We are all condemned to die
From the moment of our birth!

1987

Clay warrior

I am made immortal by my death
At that moment when there is no breath,
When the beating of my heart has stilled
And my thoughts no longer can be willed.
I was made a mortal by my birth –
At that moment when I reached the earth,
When my image fashioned out of clay
Made me just as fleeting as a day.
So transfigured I must yield to Fate,
To a predetermined time and date,
To those feelings coming from within
Reveal where all things really true begin:
Life has a birth, life even has a Fall
So expressed, it holds us all in thrall!

1987

Mozart and Kisses

In a Mozart Symphony

Passions are the violin strings,

Dangers are the oboes, horns;

And remembrance of things past,

The refrain of the flute.

With my senses so exposed,

Fate conspired to lift my soul

Through the magic of a kiss.

In a moment it revealed

Love is giving, Love is truth.

Play my passions on the strings,

Stop my senses with the winds.

As to how to still my fears?

Mozart and an endless kiss.

1988

First light

Dawn –

drawn across the sky

in fading blue and pink –

pastel.

Dawn –

light relief from night,

the promise of a day

Unveiled.

Dawn –

In my lover's eyes

Reflects a cloudfree sky

Clearblue.

Dawn –

born again it glows;

there is no end to dreams

expressed. 1988

Awakening

When does the dream become
reality?
When does reality
become the dream?
Perhaps in the dreaming
we are alive;
or is it waking
we are bereft?
The bypaths of my dreams
Lie underfoot,
Like tangled undergrowth,
Going nowhere.
The figures that intrude
Shatter on touch,
Killing the illusion
I have control.
The dreamer and the dream;

Are they the same?

The only Analyst

Is staying still.

1988

Hope

What is hope?

Hope is a dream, hope is a longing

For a cure or a treatment, or an end to the pain,

For a sunrise, at last, and the laugh of your child

For a day, for a month – perhaps for a year.

Hope is the clay from which you can shape the rest of your life.

The trigger to healing, the pathway of love,

Hope is the hand you hold on to

When you walk down the road in the dark.

(Written for Daffodil Day. September 1990)

A Near Death Happening

When I was younger, I would count the stars
Imagining that each one was a soul -
Of someone who had gone through heaven's door.
And where there was no star, I saw a hole,
An open door through which no soul could soar -
The ones that God proclaimed could not be stars.
Though I am older now I gaze at stars,
But not in awe that they and I are one,
Or that I need not die to find that place
That we call heaven, knowing I have gone
Within the Light and felt His knowing grace -
I'm freed by life eternal – there are no bars -
God smiles and shines a light so we can see
Beyond the shadows to the endless sea.

1993

* *In 1983 I experienced a Near Death Happening. This happened again in 1984.*

Jamestown, 1994

(On the street where they filmed 'High Noon')

His beady eyes were fixed on mine,
The shadow of his hat a mask
Of evil covering his face;
I watched out for the slightest sign
Of movement and did not ask
Why he had picked this dusty place.

Sonora, Jamestown, Sutter's Creek,
The gold towns of the mother lodes
Were where men came to find their wealth,
And where the lawless came to seek
Their fortune by the different codes
Of gun or by some form of stealth.

And when they saw my marshal's star

Some chose to seek their fame
By daring me to fight a duel.
They said he'd come from somewhere far,
Been paid to make the whole town tame,
And picked because they knew him cruel.

My gun was quicker than a blink,
He lay face down, he'd lost his chance
To make his mark by killing me.
The townsfolk offered me a drink
But I said thanks and held my stance;
There were more towns for me to see!
1994

I went to Gundegai

I went to Gundegai.

I wonder why

I went to Gundegai.

Because I had to go?

I don't know.

Somewhere between

Here and there

I'm not sure where

I went to Gundegai.

Don't ask me why.

It isn't here, it isn't there,

It isn't anywhere.

If you've been there

Don't tell a soul,

Sometimes the parts

Are better than the whole!! 1996

I was, I am, I will be

I was, I am, I will be.

The active parts of a sentence

Are the only ones with presence,

The only ones that describe me.

The past and future was and is

Removed from me as I am now

Between the breaks the tides allow

Before they upend all of this.

For now, I wallow in the swell

In time will stop and break this spell.

2009

Whodunnit?

Whodunnit!

Who peeled back

the pages of the calendar

and said, “That’s it!”.

Make your new resolutions

on a new page,

It’s a new year -

like the first one was

and which you

have long forgotten!

So whodunnit?

The woman

with the hourglass figure

and sand in her belly,

That’s who.

My Mother-Father Time.

2009

The edge

I stand at the edge of my extinction
At the edge of my distinction
At having survived so many times
That time itself no longer mimes
The presence of that eternity
In which I live and which I die.

I am trapped in time's undertow
The pull of which I know I know
Returns as waves upon the shore;
It's what I see, I know no more
Than that uncertainty is strife
And death still underpins all life.

For now, the flames of life still burn
To light my way on this sojourn. 2010

Not this time around

Not this time around they said.

Your life is circumscribed

But then again it may well be

This is your time around, you see.

We think of time as one straight line,

But nothing's straight, not even time.

The arc seems small, but no,

It turns, and turns, and comes again…

The ball, the wheel, this is very earth

Represents the revolution

Where intersecting lines collide

Then coalesce and unity ensues.

2010

To Max

(following your funeral)

You are not dead, you are still here,
It's just your senses have all died
And with no voice or ear or touch
Cannot communicate your fear
Of being dead and how you tried
To show you love me, and how much
You truly did not want to die.
You fought so hard to stay with me
With nose to nose and heart to heart.
Now all that I can do is cry
In sorrow that this had to be
In anguish that we are apart.

And though we cannot roll back time

My memories are all sublime!

2011

My beautiful, beautiful Max

One minute a beating heart
The next a lifeless vault;
One minute a cosmic part
The next a space-time fault.
We always knew, understood,
Communed as soul to soul -
Were together as we should
In order to be whole.
I am so sad, so, so sad
My friend has died, and died
Knowing that he should have had
Me with him by his side.
We've lost each other’s touch
That mortal link of love;
Can memories keep us much
Alive our soul of love?
In the meantime, we will mourn,

To try to ease the pain;
Knowing never can the dawn
Ever be the same again

O Max, O Max, where are you?
O Max, where are you now?
O Max, whatever you do
Or where you go, I'll know!!
You were a God-given gift
A gift of love, a joy;
In time's vast expansive drift
You anchored me, my boy.
Nose to nose and eye to eye
We knew this was our time
Together before we die
Under this eternal sky.
O Max, O Max I'm done for,
Undone within my mind
That cannot rationalize your
Leaving all this life behind.
But's best you died before me
Or who would have loved you
Quite the same. It had to be.

It's something we both knew!

I know.

2011

What’s it like, dad?

(Upon visiting the grave of my father)

What's it like?

What's it feel like?

I ask but only hear the wind,

The birds, the traffic's distant roar.

My brain tells me that you’re stone dead,

Stone deaf and cannot hear.

My heart tells me a different tale:

That you’re not here but over there.

It's a long way from Karsakiskia,

You're a long way from your home

That still stands as it was then,

And where I guess you always were!

2011

Death is expected in old age

Death is expected in old age
When the blinds are finally drawn
So no light comes through at dawn
To lighten the words of the Sage:
Death holds sway over everyone
Of any creature young or old.
Its scythe is sharp and icy cold
It renders every one to none.
We cannot dodge that fateful blow
It comes too fast and far too soon
To let us play with our balloons
As we would wish, and this we know.
So come, let's now prepare our bed
For that long sleep when we are dead.

2011

Au Revoir René

I am love consumed

As your love has burned my heart.

I'll go to my grave

With you engraved upon my heart.

I'll exit this life

With you as my lover's heart.

I'll say my goodbyes

With you as memory's heart.

This is how it ends

With you tearing at my heart.

So will I depart

This life, all lived in my heart.

2013

Euthanasia

My dear friend Clive
for me you are still
Very much alive.
You didn't wait mañana
To get the marijuana
You said it was all bliss
And better than the drugs
Supplied by all those thugs
That fried your brain
Without much gain.
The Indian roads you rode
You said were very steep
But now you'll navigate them
In your long and quiet sleep.
Rest on dear friend
The pain and fear have gone
On this you can depend

The sun at last has shone!

2017

Pain

Don't complain
About the pain;
You're still alive!
So feel the pain.
Pain reveals
And conceals;
You're still alive!
See how it feels.
Someone said
Dead is dead;
You're still alive!
Just keep your head.
And keep this thought:
Your pain was wrought.

2019

Autumn leaves

Autumn leaves are falling from the trees,
Dropping willy-nilly to the ground,
Slowly stripping down the canopy.

People die and drop down every day,
Falling, arbitrarily, to earth
As if Autumn was here all the time.

2020

Covid-19 Quarantine

Sunday, Thursday, Wednesday, Monday;
Every day feels like every other,
Blurred, except when I am jolted
Back to hearing Gambro* calling,
Saying, "Count each day you're living,
Even though the world is dying."
Yes, the sky is so much cleaner,
Quieter too, the jets are grounded;
Empty streets and with no traffic
To disturb the wary walkers
Trying to keep a social distance
From each other as they scurry.
Is this an alien invasion
Or, from excess, our punishment?
2020

*A haemodialysis machine

I Still recall that afternoon

I still recall that afternoon
In late November as I sat
Across the desk from Dr Gloom;
He clearly did not want to chat
As he described my pending doom
And told me that my end was soon.

Although it happened years ago
It's still imprinted on or my brain
As if it was just yesterday
I lost all hearing, as in vain
I hoped he'd smile and hear him say
"I'm wrong, you still have years to go."

It's 2020 as I write
While all about me all the world

Is sitting on a precipice;
A virus strain has been unfurled
And threatens to envelope us
And no one has been spared this blight

So every day is like that day -
That day is 1983
When I was told my time was up.
So far the fates have nurtured me,
And always somehow filled my cup,
And kept me safe upon my way.

I'm not so vain as to believe
I'll live forever and withstand
The constant challenges I face.
But this I know that while I live
I'll keep my options close at hand
And choose those acts I can embrace.
2020

Rescue

The time is fast approaching when
The world will start to breathe again;
For far too long its held its breath
For fear it would inhale its death –
That long release from all the pain
And from this plague brought on by men.

My mother braved the Spanish flu,
And talked how people round her fell;
Now I'm reminded of that time
As I attempt to find the rhyme
That helps me through to break the spell
Of what I have been going through.

It's in this time-approaching scene
I'll soon receive my first vaccine!
2021

Life, death and passing through

ISBN: 978-0-646-83273-9

Born and educated in South Africa, Joel taught English at a private high school before embarking on a successful career as a creative director in advertising until his first cancer diagnosis at age 43.

Despite several life-threatening medical challenges, he worked as a psychotherapist, published three books, and founded a national not-for-profit organization to help patients and their doctors better manage the psychosocial and existential issues of cancer and other life-threatening illnesses. In recognition of this work, he was awarded the Order of Australia Medal in 2008.

ISBN 978-0-646-83273-9

9 780646 832739 >

Printed in Great Britain
by Amazon

56221645R00193